(Mary) Jenny,

May these virtal
truths enrich your life,

Olga

VITAL
TRUTHS

VITAL
TRUTHS

THE SECRET TO LIVING AND
LEADING WHOLEHEARTEDLY

BRUCE E. ROSELLE, PHD

Beaver's Pond Press, Inc.
Edina, Minnesota

ISBN 1-931646-81-3

Library of Congress Catalog Number: 2002112080

06 05 04 03 02   6 5 4 3 2 1

Beaver's Pond Press, Inc.

7104 Ohms Lane, Suite 216
Edina, MN 55439-1465
(952) 829-8818
www.beaverspondpress.com

to order, visit www.BookHouseFulfillment.com or call 1-800-901-3480. Reseller discounts available.

For all of us who strive every day
to set aside our self-focused tendencies
in order to lead wholehearted lives.

CONTENTS

VITAL –

Existing as a manifestation of life;
necessary to the maintenance of life;
full of life and vigor.

TRUTHS –

The real state of affairs;
sincere character, action, and speech;
the quality or state of being faithful.

FOREWORD

Particularly in the last decade of my nearly 30–year career, I have become aware of how often we are the biggest obstacle to our own energy and effectiveness. My work during this period has focused mostly on executive coaching, psychological assessment, leadership development training, and organizational intervention. The spark to write this book came out of my own stumbling journey on the path toward wholeheartedness, as well as the perspective I gained through deep dialogue with individuals I have coached and trained.

The biggest breakthrough in my thinking came when I was asked to create a session on life balance for human resource managers. I agreed to do it, but soon realized that I was sick to death of the whole concept of balance because it always seemed like such an impossible struggle. After sitting and looking at the computer screen for what seemed like hours, I finally looked up "balance" in the dictionary. The definition revolved around a difficult choice between two or more competing forces. Suddenly I understood why balance always seemed like a struggle—by its very definition it involves deciding for one thing and against another!

I searched my heart for a different word and came up with "abundance." What people really want, I realized, is a full, abundant life that works. I considered further the aspects of an abundant life and the people I knew who live their lives out of an attitude of abundance rather than an attitude of scarcity. It was then that I recognized a certain "wholeheartedness" in the lives of these people that was—at the deepest level—an attitude toward life and relationships. I began to consider the foundation of this wholehearted attitude and eventually identified a total of seven elements of wholeheartedness. These became the vital truths described in this book.

My hope and prayer for you, the reader of this book, is that you will recognize the vital nature of these truths and the importance of building them into your life right now. This is not a self-help book filled with unique and novel ideas you've never thought of or tried before. Instead, it is designed to bring you back to the bedrock of what makes life worth living and leading. It is filled with truths your heart already knows but has lost sight of. May it be for you, as it has been for me, the beginning of a life-changing journey on a path that leads to a more wholehearted life for you and all those whose lives you touch.

WHOLEHEARTED –
Undivided in purpose,
enthusiasm, or will.

1 | INTRODUCTION: THE TRUTH ABOUT BEING WHOLEHEARTED

A colleague of mine described a holiday family gathering that occurred years ago at which she first met a distant, relative known to the world as Supreme Court Justice Warren Burger. She described his presence in a room of people as "grace personified," and told of how he focused on each individual he met as if he or she was the only person in the room.

Later, when he was asked to tell stories about the presidents, generals, and foreign heads of state he had met and known over the years, Burger talked about them in such a way that the focus remained on the people he had met, not on himself. There was something about Warren Burger's attitude that drew people to him and kept them at his side.

Many people in leadership roles—whether they lead thousands or just themselves—miss the true importance of developing a wholehearted attitude that permeates all aspects of their lives. The popular business media have in recent years illustrated the difficulty organizational leaders experience in maintaining a wholehearted attitude outside the office. We have read about, for example, the broken marriages as well as the psychologically scarred sons and daughters of senior managers and executives in major corporations. These are executives who understand the importance of exhibiting the competencies and character of leaders in their formal business roles, but somehow miss the truth about developing a wholehearted attitude with their families.

The nonbusiness media have illuminated the dark, ugly truths of the private lives of televangelists, athletic heroes, world leaders, and others who provide formal and informal leadership to millions around the world. These are people who, for the most part, exhibit many of the competencies and character traits of leaders while engaged in their formal roles, but who fail miserably in other important leadership roles in their lives.

I believe that these leaders have failed to carry the mantle of leadership in all aspects of their lives because their hearts have been divided. They have failed to recognize the vital truth that they carry the same heart into all facets of their lives, and that to be truly effective in all their leadership roles their hearts must not be fragmented. Their hearts must be as whole and consistent as possible across all roles, all events, and every word out of their mouths. This is as true for those who are simply leading their own lives as it is for national and corporate leaders.

A couple of stories may help illustrate the importance of both living and leading wholeheartedly. Tom is the vice president of marketing for a large financial services organization. He has a number of important leadership roles at home and in the community. From his own description, his wife is devoted to him and relies on him to make the most important decisions for their family of five. They are both committed Christians and very active in their parish. Tom serves on the board of deacons and teaches Sunday school. His three children are well adjusted, know that their parents love them, and look forward to Dad's presence and occasional coaching at their sporting and musical events.

By all accounts, Tom is devoted and wholehearted in his roles of father, husband, church leader, and son to his aging parents. In his role as marketing leader in his company, however, he is seen much differently. People in multi-rater feedback described him as competitive and combative, someone who seems to have only his own interests in mind. They depicted him as an intellectual gatekeeper who squelched new ideas, aggressively questioned and challenged perspectives that differed from his own, and refused to carry out directives with which he disagreed. Because his boss tended to encourage what he viewed as "healthy debate," and because his bullying tactics cowed others on the senior team, his behavior went unchallenged.

How does someone like Tom develop such separate lives between work and home? How could someone with such strong leadership competencies and character traits at home and in the community become such a tyrant at work?

The complement to Tom's situation is Gloria, a highly successful home-based network marketer. In leading her business, Gloria is viewed by those upstream in the hierarchy as the future of the organization. Her ideas not only motivate those who sell through her, but help create the vision that will propel the organization into a new level of growth. She is a breath of fresh air to those who work around her because of her contagious energy, humor, and compassion for them. The customers and her network contacts love her because she tells them the truth and delivers on what she promises.

The family part of home, however, is a different situation altogether. Her first marriage ended in a contentious divorce in which she was given custody of the children. Her children are now teenagers; the oldest has been involved with drugs, was struggling with the relevance of school, and has made at least one unsuccessful attempt at suicide. The youngest did well in school, but tended to be a loner and spent quite a bit of time in front of the television or on the Internet. Because of Gloria's heavy time commitment to customers, up-line and down-line network contacts, and conferences, the kids often take care of themselves nights and mornings during the school week.

In Gloria's case, her leadership is wholehearted for the most part in her work, but her business commitment leaves little motivation to be much of a positive leader with her family. Her beliefs about the importance of being wholehearted are inconsistent across her various roles, with the most evidence of this divided heart appearing in her role as mother. The lack of wholeheartedness in her leadership role at home also occasionally spills over into her business, stealing energy and enthusiasm from that part of her life.

Our lives do not need to be like Tom's or Gloria's, with us being very different people in our work and in our family interactions. It is possible to be a wholehearted leader in all aspects of our lives. Developing a fundamentally wholehearted attitude—one that is evident regardless of the circumstances—is where true leadership begins.

What does it look like when someone lives and leads wholeheartedly? A wholehearted leader is one whose attitude is contagious in its enthusiasm, whose heart is pure in its intent, and whose will is undivided in its purpose. Attitudes are beliefs that motivate behavior. Wholehearted leaders believe in the vital truths described in this book and live their life with an attitude of abundance that colors their work, family, and community involvement. The intentions of their heart are as pure as is humanly possible. They are clear about their purpose in each situation, without internal confusion and doubt. People who approach life with this kind of attitude are able to focus wholeheartedly on each moment of it, to live and lead their lives fully and completely.

To lead wholeheartedly is to lead with a positive attitude and a big–picture perspective on issues at all levels at home and at work. It reflects a bedrock belief that the best way to get your own needs met is by focusing on the success of others, setting appropriate boundaries, and living life with a long-range view. It is to live according to the vital truths presented in the next seven chapters so that the wholehearted spirit can be set free. Because of their contagious attitude of enthusiasm, energy, and confidence, these people are drawn into leadership roles and attract others as followers. Others recognize their wholehearted attitude and trust them in a way that self-focused leaders never experience.

The purpose of this book is to help you develop yourself and those around you into the kind of leader whose heart is whole and consistent. Living and leading wholeheartedly is a lifelong commitment that involves a continuous shaping of attitude, heart, and will. It is a learning process that approaches but never quite attains perfection. It is a path that leads to greater joy and fulfillment in your work and life. While the seven vital truths of wholehearted leadership are defined and described uniquely in this book, they are based on experience, ancient wisdom, biblical truth, and even common sense. They are based on the truth about the kind of attitude that makes human beings more effective with other human beings.

This book is dedicated to creating a fundamental shift in your attitude so that you can become a more effective leader in all aspects of your life. If you are not on a wholehearted path right now, these words are designed to encourage you to take the first steps. If you have been on the path but have slipped, the stories here are intended to draw you back. This book will help you in the vitally important goal of becoming a wholehearted leader at work, at home, and in your community. All of us are leaders, whether or not we hold the formal title of leadership. By following the perspective and approach suggested in this book, we can live and lead wholeheartedly through every role we fill in our lives.

The first thing in life is to do with a purpose what one proposes to do.

—*Pablo Casals*

2 | KNOW THE PURPOSE IN WHAT YOU PROPOSE TO DO

For most of us, life is full of choices that consume portions of our daily allotment of hours. No matter how hard we try and how quickly new technology allows us to process information and automate tasks, we still only have 24 hours in any day and 168 hours in a week. The various modes we can choose for communicating—phone, pager, e-mail, voice mail, facsimile, face-to-face, letters, Web page—give us some small picture of how overwhelming the choices are that we face every day of our lives. How do we decide where to devote our life's time? On what basis can we choose?

We are also deluged on a daily basis with information and points of view from so many sources—radio, television, video/DVD, people, CD–ROM, Internet, books, faxes, phone calls—we do not know who or what to believe anymore. Radio talk shows, television news magazines, celebrity inter-views/interviewers such as Bill O'Reilly, Oprah, Geraldo, Letterman, and other media provide us with so many opin-ions that it is difficult to know what to think. How do we know what to believe or where to draw the line?

To use a listening analogy, we have too much noise in our lives and not nearly enough signal. When the noise around us becomes so loud that we can no longer hear a particular voice, for example, then what is genuine becomes difficult to distinguish from what is artificial, and truth becomes hard to separate from falsehood. We each need some sort of screening device that helps us decide what to choose and how to spend our life's time. We need perspective. We need to know the purpose in what we propose to do. Having perspective is knowing your purpose and aligning your life to it.

Perspective on our own lives provides us with two critical elements in separating the signal from the noise. The first element is purpose, the sense of mission or calling that determines the priority of relationships, situations, and opportunities. The second is context, the ability to look at relationships, situations, and opportunities with a frame of reference that determines the criticality of each. Both context and purpose are central to perspective, and perspective is foundational to wholehearted leadership.

The perspective that purpose offers to us on a daily basis is the set of reasons to either choose or not choose to spend our life's time and energy in a particular endeavor. Purpose helps us decide why we make life choices. Purpose is not just an abstract concept, but something to be defined, understood, and referred to every day. Until we take the time and focus to explore our purpose, we will not discover true joy in our work or contentment with what we have.

The question we must answer that addresses our purpose and gives us perspective is, "Why do I do what I do in my life?" Just as the mission statement for an organization answers the question of why it exists in the marketplace, so too our purpose statement answers the "why" question. Having a clear sense of our own purpose that we know to be true in our heart is the only template we can have for making the difficult decisions about how to spend our life's time.

Historically, the meaning of perspective—purpose and context—centered on vocation or a life calling from God. Our English word "vocation" comes from the Latin word *vocare,* which means "to call." Being called to a purpose is different than being driven. Driven people tend to seek accomplishment for the wrong reasons—power or self-promotion. Or they are urged on by deeper, internal motives such as an irrational need for significance or a desire to please or impress others. When we slip into a driven mode, our lives take on a quality that some might describe as joyless and brittle. Nothing seems very satisfying in this mode because being driven has a way of beating the life out of us.

When we are genuinely living out our God-given vocation—responding to the calling in our lives—our experience is quite different. Many people today still define their purpose as a calling to do God's will, to do what God created and equipped them to do. As one person described his purpose to me, it was "to live in God's light, love, and service." These people believe that every organism in the universe has an intelligently designed purpose that determines its function and role. People who have this sense of perspective determine for themselves what God's will is by first studying his word to learn the true nature of God and then seeking his direction through prayer and contemplation. Those who look to God for a sense of purpose are typically brought to a crisis of belief in which they become uncertain and confused. It is in responding to this crisis that they must adjust their lives to more completely obey what they perceive God's will to be.

This certainly was the situation with Peter, an operational vice president for a large manufacturing organization. I worked with Peter for the better part of a year to help him become more effective in his role. He had recently received some pretty clear feedback that really shocked him—others in his department did not trust him, did not view him as someone who listened well or valued other perspectives. They perceived him to be highly competitive and inflexible in his approach, as well as someone who would not take responsibility for his mistakes.

Early on in our coaching relationship, Peter told me that he was a committed Christian and wanted our work together to focus in part on how to live out his religious principles both at home and at work. That is, he wanted to make certain that he was living his life according to God's purpose. By the end of our coaching, he had turned around the distrust by others, had become a person who listened without drifting or interrupting, and was viewed as a valued team player. Shortly after our coaching ended, however, he also came to the conclusion that his job was not where God intended him to be. He decided that he would enroll in divinity school, complete his degree, and then enter the ministry full time. And he was very excited about this new perspective on the context and purpose of his life.

Much of contemporary thinking, contrary to Peter's, focuses on purpose as a life objective or goal that individuals determine solely from within themselves. This perspective is not rooted in the context of vocation but is based on a belief in the power of our potential as human beings to determine our own direction, set our own course, and to fulfill our own sense of purpose. This perspective holds that the universe itself is purposeful in its nature, and that a critical part of our development is the search for purpose and meaning that starts on the inside and works its way out.

Within this way of determining purpose, I have met and worked with individuals who defined their purpose in various ways, including the following:

- Self—to support myself independently, be all that I can be
- Family—to be the best provider for my family, to serve them
- Principles/values—to live by truth, justice, and brotherly love

To illustrate the purpose based on self, John was a young man working at a car dealership where I test-drove a car I was considering leasing. As we took off in the vehicle, John looked wistfully around at the leather interior of the vehicle, and confided to me that "my life goal is to own a car like this!" I studied his face as carefully as I could while driving an unfamiliar car down an unfamiliar road to determine whether he was being sincere, or just trying to sell me on the car.

Then I realized that his comments illustrated the self-purpose statement of "making enough money to support myself independently," or own a nice car, rent a great apartment, etc. Aspiring to own a nice car is enough to get a young man or woman out of bed in the morning, cleaned up, and off to work for eight hours a day. Once the car is achieved, however, a new purpose objective must be identified. Here are some other specific examples of how people I have interviewed define purpose in terms of self:

- Make enough money to pay my bills, get out of debt, retire early, etc.

- Continually improve myself, learn new things, live up to my potential
- Live life to the fullest with no regrets, face new challenges, travel, etc.
- Obtain and keep peace of mind, be happy, have fun at whatever I do
- Be a good person, to grow in everything I do

Many people I have worked with over the years have had as their purpose to be the best provider they can be for their families. Both men and women often view parenting as their prominent role and therefore the core of their life purpose. Work, for example, is seen within the framework of "being the best provider for my family." That is why they work; it is what gets them out of bed in the morning. This is a bigger context than making enough money to be independent because it involves other people in the family and it is more likely to last a lifetime, with perhaps a shift in later years to being "the best grandparent I can be." Some examples of this kind of purpose statement include the following:

- Provide a better life for my family, keep them happy, safe, fulfilled
- Support my kids to get the best education, succeed in life, contribute to society
- Be a good parent, a role model for my children
- Love and be loved, leave a legacy of love for children

An even larger context can be created by those who define their purpose in terms of fundamental principles. The context for these purpose statements is often beyond self and family/friends, and may include some sort of lasting impact. Like purpose statements shaped around self or family, these provide a frame of reference that gives meaning and direction to life. They give people a template that helps them say yes to some activities and no to others, based on how well aligned these activities are to their sense of life purpose. Some examples of this type of purpose statement include:

- Help others, be a care provider to those in need, share with and care for them
- Mentor others, help them grow, develop, feel good about themselves
- Affect positive change in the community, schools, churches, etc.
- Provide opportunities for people to explore, expand, and demonstrate their self-knowledge

These various purpose statements can be viewed as concentric circles that get bigger in scope and longer in time. The smallest circle, for example, would be one that focuses just on the individual for a limited time. "Make enough money to pay my bills," is an example of such a circle. As the perspective takes on a longer time frame and encompasses a broader scope, it becomes more powerful. Examples here would include, "Support my kids to get the best education," or "Be

a good person, to grow in everything I do." The biggest circles of perspective last a lifetime and provide a continuous
sense of meaning and direction. Statements such as "Affect
positive change in the community," or "Help others, be a care
provider for those in need," are examples of ones that could
last a lifetime.

Still other purpose statements can sound lofty but have little
capacity to provide a daily sense of meaning and purpose in
life. For example, when you think of your purpose as something like, "To be happy," "To be a good person," or "To live
life to the fullest," you will have problems day to day deciding which choices are most likely to take you a step closer to
your purpose. The most effective purpose statements provide
both meaning and direction, and last a lifetime.

Many purpose statements can seem to shift their meaning in
times of crisis. For more than a decade, I had helped managers
and executives find new jobs and careers after they had been
right–sized, merged, or acquisitioned out of jobs. What happens to these people when their purpose is "Being the best
provider for my family?" It gets dramatically buffeted and
banged around during the job search/transition process and
sometimes never fully recovers. This is one reason why so
many people in career transition take the time to reevaluate
their life purpose and career thinking. Often they identify a
new purpose that is broader, deeper, or significantly different

from the one that had guided them for the first 20 years of their careers.

Sometimes purpose attached to the family takes on a rather vague or impossible–to–achieve feeling. When I asked 50-year-old Bill what his life purpose was, he responded, "To make my family happy." This got him out of the bed in the morning and down the hall to his home-based business office, but it also created some complications. Whenever one's purpose is attached to the emotional state of others, there is potential for problems. What if they don't want to be happy? What if they won't let you make them happy? Happy is both a vague feeling and a generally impossible emotional state to create in other people if they are not already inclined in that direction.

Other times, life circumstances and situations can threaten to undermine one's sense of purpose. Sarah, for example, is a person who perceives her life purpose as bringing love to others. She defines love as unconditional love, the kind that the Greeks termed "agape." Through her work as a marriage and family therapist, and her roles as mother, wife, sibling, and daughter, she lives her life as much as possible with the purpose of bringing love and acceptance into the lives of others. Her clients experience the healing balm of her life purpose, and her children and siblings know that she will be the one to reach out to them if something gets in the way of the relationship.

Periodically, however, Sarah struggles with her own need for love from those around her. Always being the one to carry the cool cup of water to others over time leaves her feeling parched and thirsty to receive this same kind of love. When her husband becomes distant and aloof or her children react in rebellious and angry ways, her sense of purpose is threatened and her bucket of agape develops a hole that is difficult for her to plug.

Several years ago, a participant in a wholehearted leadership workshop asked me what my purpose was. I realized that I had not actually written it out in the way that I had been asking people to do in these sessions! I opened my mouth to respond to her question, and out came the words, "To help people grow and develop to their fullest capacity." Today, this purpose statement continues to guide my fathering of two teenagers, helps me support my wife in her needs, directs the services I choose to provide through my business, and provides a focus for my volunteer commitments at my church and in my community. I also apply it to myself so that, for example, I welcome—most of the time—the new growth edges my wife points out to me.

The Perspective of Wholehearted Leaders

Throughout the remaining chapters of this book, we will look more closely at various combinations of individuals who are wholehearted leaders in their work, their home and in their community involvement. In the organizations with which I regularly consult, I have met many individuals who function as wholehearted leaders. The individuals featured in the following chapters are those whom I have gotten to know particularly well. It is clear to me that they are wholehearted in the various roles they play in their life. It is for this reason that I use them to help illuminate each of the seven vital truths of living and leading wholeheartedly.

Rob Stevenson, president of People Management of Minnesota, a small management consulting and executive search firm, describes his purpose as "an evolving perspective." His thoughts about purpose began during the trial–and–error period of his late twenties, which led to some "wrong and dangerous" circumstances in his finances and in his most important relationships. On the verge of losing a million dollars in a failing Porsche dealership, Rob reached out desperately to a business competitor for counsel. Instead of business advice, his competitor told Rob that business success was not as important as the beliefs that guided one's life. He asked Rob, "What do you believe?" and shared his own beliefs about purpose and life.

The impact if this conversation led Rob to what he describes as a conversion, that has evolved over the years into a purpose statement of "To know God, to love him, and to receive love from him." Living out this purpose has led Rob to a realignment of his life, starting with eliminating harmful habits like smoking and moving into changes in ways of thinking that had become inconsistent with his life purpose. The refining process continues to this day in Rob's life, which he describes as "an apprenticeship process in which you never quite fully get there."

Jim Warner, associate pastor at Hosanna! Lutheran Church, also describes his purpose in terms of God's will for his life. He views his purpose every day as "To reach out to others, to serve them, to help them, and share myself with them." This sense of purpose is based on his belief that interpersonal relationships are eternal and lasting, and that everything aside from relationships is ultimately futile and meaningless. As Jim describes it, all the time, money, and energy he spends day to day has to do with people.

The owner of a small human resources and search firm called HR Connection, Bob Bemel is a wholehearted leader who believes that being of service grounds him and fills a huge personal need. In his nonwork hours, he delivers food to shut-ins as a part of the Meals on Wheels program. He knows that when he delivers a meal to a particular 90-year-old woman who squeezes his hand as he leaves that "it means she is thankful and she is dying." Indicating that he would like to spend more time in the future purely in the service of others, Bob described his purpose in life. "To create a space where something of real value occurs as a service to others." Creating "spaces of value" is what his HR Connection small group discussions are all about, as well as the cabin he recently purchased to create a permanent gathering place for his extended family.

As discussed in the beginning of this section, having perspective is not only knowing your purpose in life but also putting things into a context. Bob illustrates this second component by recognizing that the human resource executives and managers in his groups need to step away from the day-to-day grind of the profession. "It's hard to really get perspective and focus when we're caught up in the activity of providing for self and family," he notes.

For Chuck Slocum, a management consultant with expertise in institutional leadership, purpose is developed over a period of time and life experiences. "You get comfortable with who you are over time, and then God speaks to us through the doors that are opened about what we should be doing with our lives," he said. Having functioned as an executive at businesses such as Honeywell and Dayton Hudson, as well as nonprofits such as the Arthritis Foundation and Minnesota Business Partnership, Chuck has been in the consulting arena for 10 years. He defines his purpose in life as "Being an impact leader" for the organizations he serves. Outside of work, he functions as an impact leader at his church, in his role on various boards, and in his most significant relationships—with his wife, Francelle, and the young man he mentors as part of the Life Coaches program for father-absent children.

Even with the limitations of some of the purpose statements illustrated earlier in this chapter, simply having a sense of purpose has enriched the lives of each of these people. Further, the leadership they have been able to exercise in the various roles of their life has been powerfully augmented. The more encompassing the purpose statement, the more deeply held the convictions associated with it, and the less self-focused it is, the more wholehearted will be the leadership in all aspects of one's life. Those people who have a firm sense of perspective in their life tend to focus their vision on the long-term, show persistence in the face of obstacles, be patient when things go wrong in the short-term, and live up to their commitments.

Having a clear sense of purpose in life gives us the perspective to choose where we will focus our energies and the resolve to finish well—to bring our activities to conclusion. Without the foundation of purposeful alignment, life choices can become confusing, shallow, and at times paralyzing. Individuals without a clear sense of purpose tend to start and drop things over and over in life. They tend to be uncertain about decisions they make and less than fully committed.

People without a long-term, life-long perspective tend to bail out of agreements, feel frustration with the results they are achieving, and continually shift the focus of their energy. They tend to experience few moments in which their hearts and minds are wholeheartedly focused.

Perspective is a critical element of wholehearted leadership in your various life roles. Take some time right now to think about your own sense of purpose in life. Is it clearly defined in your mind? Does your heart get excited when you think about your purpose? What is the vital truth about your life purpose? Using insights from this chapter and other sources, take the time soon to write down some initial ideas related to your purpose.

Nothing great was ever achieved without enthusiasm.
—Ralph Waldo Emerson

3 | GENERATE ENTHUSIASM TO ACHIEVE GREAT THINGS

We read and hear words such as "motivation" and "motivated" every day in our culture. Health centers, weight loss and diet gurus, and self-improvement experts urge us to "get motivated." We are exposed to motivational speakers at work and in the media. Advertisements for a wide variety of consumer products urge us in one way or another to "just do it."

Motivation would not be such a hot commodity these days if we as individuals actually were highly motivated. The truth is that in spite of the very high general standard of living and health in our society, we struggle daily to generate enough energy to just get motivated, much less stay motivated. We are faced with a motivation crisis in our culture today. We desperately want to feel energized by and enthused about our work and our lives, but we cannot seem to generate this energy and enthusiasm on our own. And the books, videos, and audio tapes that urge us to lighten up, take our job and love it, or float our own boat have mostly provided a Band-Aid of techniques. The problem is that we have lost the key to our own motivation.

Organizations struggle to generate enthusiasm in their employees and to retain them over time. Too many people are just going through the motions in their lives, rushing to get things done before the day ends or trying to stay awake long enough to punch out. Either way, they handle their employment and family responsibilities by doling out a minimal amount of energy to each one so that they do not run out before the end of the day or week. Individuals who have left corporate employment and started entrepreneurial ventures and home-based businesses tend to begin with a great amount of motivation and energy, but struggle to maintain these in the face of marketplace and resource challenges.

Most people have very little insight about what really motivates them in their work and life. Many have become disconnected from what gives them the most joy and have focused instead on what will make them the most money. Money is a short-term motivator, but seldom continues to energize in the long run. In my own career, I left a senior psychologist position at a major university to join an organizational consulting firm. In the process, my salary actually doubled. This was very exciting to me for about two months, at which point I began to think of this new salary as my actual "worth"—and the motivational value of it dropped off precipitously. Over the years when I have polled people to determine what is most motivating for them in their work, money was typically about fifth on the list.

If money is not the most powerful motivator in our work lives, what is? Again from my research, work characteristics like being involved in decision-making, being able to accomplish tasks as they choose, and having coworkers who are friends were typically strong motivators. Engaging in work that feeds these needs results in a more satisfying work life.

Other factors are important as well. In addition to having insight about characteristics of work that energize us, it is important to understand what motivates us personally and deeply about work. The greater your insight about who you are, how you are designed, and in what ways you are uniquely talented—and the more you use this insight to structure your work and life—the more energized you will become. The greater degree to which your work and nonwork activities tap into your underlying motivations and talents, the greater will be your energy. The truth about motivation is that you must purposely engage in work and activities that use your unique, innate talents.

We are each intricately and intelligently designed. That design includes our own particular talents and abilities, the DNA combination that is uniquely ours. Out of that design come some enduring patterns of thinking and behavior that have motivated us in the past and will continue to energize us in the future. We can each look back, for example, at the peak moments in our lives and identify what motivates and energizes us most completely.

Using an approach like this, I discovered a number of years ago that what most motivated me in my work and life was to have an impact on people through my ideas. In the past, I have conveyed these ideas through a variety of media—painting, songwriting, writing, presenting, and coaching—and each of these have been and continue to motivate and energize me. This represents an enduring, unchanging pattern of what motivates me most in my work and life.

Fortunately, not everybody has the same need to have an impact through ideas like I do—or nobody would ever ask me what I think! Instead, we all have very different combinations of underlying needs. Some people need to compete and become the best in their area of expertise, while others are drawn to overcoming major challenges. Still others are motivated to build organizations or structures, or to bring a unique concept to life. Some people are excited about speaking to and influencing an audience; others would prefer to do research and write up the results. Some like to work with their hands and be physically active; others like to interpret subtle nuances through painting and photography.

When I have asked people what is most motivating to them in their work and life, the following are typical of the kinds of activities they shared with me:

- Solving interesting problems, working on challenging projects

- Making changes that have a clearly positive impact, that improve processes
- Creating an energizing work environment for others
- Working on multiple tasks at the same time
- Completing projects, having a sense of accomplishment
- Organizing and structuring a situation
- Envisioning and planning improvements
- Having an opportunity to be creative, to use humor, have fun
- Working with others toward a common goal
- Helping another learn, improve, grow, develop

This list represents what might be called motivated abilities that these people recognize in themselves. A couple of examples of individuals I have coached might help make the concept of motivated abilities even clearer. Benjamin was the senior sales executive for a pharmaceutical manufacturer. He had spent a couple of frustrating years trying to move his CEO and his peers in a particular business direction, only to be constantly rebuffed and ultimately let go by the organization. When we first met, Benjamin was tense, defensive, and not at all clear why his last situation had not worked out. He completed a motivated abilities pattern assessment to help him decide what to do next with his life. When we looked at his pattern, it indicated that the primary result he wanted to achieve is to advance and be key to propelling his group in new directions.

He smiled and looked relieved as he recognized himself. It was clear to him then that his last position was not a situation in which he had failed, but rather a situation that happened to be a very bad fit with his primary motivations. Benjamin saw also that being with people and having a responsible role was critical to his satisfaction. He recognized that a work environment in which he could start something from scratch, work collaboratively, and apply what he knows was the ideally motivating situation. The last time I met with Benjamin and his wife, he had just landed his first large client in a new, home-based consulting business. He was happy and energized, and his wife looked at him with love and respect as he described his new "position."

David, the president of a regional banking center, was motivated in a very different way. Our discussions indicated that the primary result he wanted to achieve in his career was to make tangible certain ideals and values in order to make a difference. It was important to him to be making a difference in his role, and to do it in a way that could be seen as "right" by some external standard. Our conversations also focused on the fact he was very energized by having major responsibilities in an organization, by seeing others grow and reach their potential, and by working with new, state-of-the-art methods. He saw that he was not a strongly detail-oriented person and worked best when he functioned as the engineer or prime mover of an initiative.

Unfortunately for David, the role he was in when we first met did not pull strongly on these motivated abilities. His presidential role required him to gently massage the differing agendas of members of his board of directors. Their focus, as well as that of the CEO and CFO, was primarily on the bottom line. They showed very little interest in whether the organization was strongly values driven or making a distinctive mark in the financial arena. They did not recognize the importance of David's people growing into their potential unless it directly impacted profitability.

These insights led David to seek a different role within his broader organizational structure. It was a role that provided a much better fit because it was a part of the business where his service-oriented approach was valued, and where he could make a tangible difference.

From these brief vignettes and from your own parallel life experiences, hopefully you recognize how important it is to know what motivates you and to build as much of it as possible into your work. The truth is that work situations and activities that do not allow you to exercise your motivated abilities will drain psychological energy without replacing it. You will feel somewhere between vaguely and acutely aware of your lack of satisfaction, but will have limited understanding of why you generate so little energy at work.

Like Benjamin, David, and me, the key is to come to some understanding of how you are designed motivationally, what energizes you day to day, and how to tap into this enthusiasm at work. The further away you are from your true motivated abilities in your work, the less energy and enthusiasm you will experience in it. And this is true whether you work for yourself or in a large organization.

Enthusiasm of Wholehearted Leaders

For Rob Stevenson, president of People Management of Minnesota, helping people identify their motivations is a way of life. His organization is part of an international group that uses the System for Identifying Motivated Abilities (SIMA) to search for and place people in appropriate organizational positions. It seemed only fair to ask him to share his own motivated ability pattern, since assessing others on their patterns is what he does for living. He described his personal pattern as "fast movement toward a goal, extracting and realizing untapped potential in relationships and groups of people."

Using a golfing analogy, Rob describes this motivation in general as like the "sweet spot" on the clubface—the place where you need the least energy to create the greatest performance. To go through life ignorant of your motivated abilities results in a great deal of "hooking and slicing" with little awareness of the fundamental motivational flaws that cause you to miss your sweet spot. Knowing his motivated abilities as thoroughly as he does, Rob recognizes that these patterns are irresistible and there is nothing he can do to dramatically change them. Like each of us, his task is to recognize and understand his motivated pattern, embrace it, and make good choices about how to direct and manage this inborn drive. He knows that his pattern tends to be expansive, with few natural limits inherent in it, so he needs to surround himself with people who can help create boundaries.

Trudy Canine, founder and owner of Pathfinders, a four-person career transition and coaching firm, found the joy in her work through a very different avenue. Her journey toward self–understanding began with an early corporate mentor who told her that she was an incredibly bright and talented person who needed to choose what she really wanted to do in her career, and then make it happen. His comments "fanned the flames" of her confidence and motivated her to look for what she really wanted to do in that organization—to find a role that really made her come alive. "Once I found the direction I wanted," she continued, "he taught me the art of 'schmoozing' and coached me on the 'street smart' kinds of things I needed to know." Trudy credits this man and his belief in her as the key to unlocking the power of her own imagination and believing that what she imagined was possible.

Later in her career, the victim of downsizing at her company, Trudy again faced the question of what really energized her and what to do next in her career. She was drawn to starting her own business and feeding her entrepreneurial side, but felt uncertain and afraid. Her husband, Jim, came along side of her and quietly asked, "Why couldn't you do it?" This simple question gave her the encouragement she needed to build a structure around the dream she had. Now, she is doing what she loves for her work, using her unique, innate talents within the context of the independence she deeply needs.

Barry Brottlund is a commercial real estate consultant and broker who has been on his own in business for nearly 27 years. Most of that time, he has worked out of an office in his home. He chose commercial real estate in the first place because of the unlimited income potential, but discovered that his primary satisfaction came from the opportunity to work with a wide range of people.

In his role, he is often the person pulling together the disparate perspectives and personalities of engineers, architects, developers, and retailers to make a project move forward. Moreover, he is energized by the variety in his work, which comes primarily through needing to know and learn about many different kinds of businesses, the people in them, and what motivates each person. "If you're able to identify your gifts and talents, and build them into your work, then the energy and passion are there because you are doing something you're able to do well," according to Barry.

Chuck Slocum "spent a lot of years trying to be a big guy in some organization" before he came to the realization of what he really loves to do and how best to present this to the marketplace. "You are your own most important client," he said. "If you can't figure out how to present yourself, how can you help others?" Out of his own self-searching and the push-back of the marketplace, Chuck has identified these four things "I love to do:"

- Ramp up quickly with a high impact plan (where are you, where do you want to be?)
- Take a project or an whole organization and execute all or part of the plan
- Identify creative new avenues of resourcing or rethinking current avenues
- Turn a failing organization around by joining them onsite for a period of time, leaving them in better shape than he found them.

Knowing what sparks his energy helps Chuck decide which projects to accept and which ones not to pursue as he continues to develop his business.

These four wholehearted leaders tell very different stories about their work life, but share a deep belief in discovering their own unique and innate talents and then pursuing them with passion. All four leaders draw others to them simply by being enthusiastic in their work and in their close relationships. They attract clients, friends, and potential professional colleagues through their obvious joy in the work they do. They are aware of what motivates them, and comfortable with who they are and who they are not.

How can you begin to identify what motivates you in your work and life? The first step is to recall the 10 most enjoyable and satisfying achievement experiences from across your lifespan, starting as early as you can remember in childhood and ending with today. For each, write down or just think about how you got involved in the activity, what your specific role and participation included, and what was most satisfying about the experience.

As you consider how you got involved and what your specific role and responsibilities were, think of the primary action verbs that describe how you accomplished the activity. It might help to imagine you are somebody else who was there with you during a particular enjoyable achievement, and describe yourself from their perspective. The pattern of the verbs you use to describe a lifetime of achievements will help you identify those abilities—like learning, speaking, evaluating, planning, organizing, influencing, constructing—that you are most motivated to use.

I don't think of all the misery but of the beauty that still remains.

—*Anne Frank*

4 | FOCUS ON THE BEAUTY THAT REMAINS

Even in times of wealth, prosperity, and happiness, it is often too easy to focus on the gap between what we have and what we want. In times of poverty, lack, and misery, it can feel impossible to focus on the beauty that remains. But whole-hearted leaders know that it is precisely in these times of emotional or financial scarcity that we must appreciate the beauty and find deep in ourselves a spirit of thankfulness. Thankfulness is the art of believing that your most important needs and desires have already been met, in spite of the circumstances surrounding you. It is within the practiced capacity to be thankful that every thorn has its rose, every rain cloud holds the potential for new growth.

Thanking others is something most of us learned as children. Our automatic response to Mom or Dad posing the question, "What do you say?" was always the phrase "Thank you!" Whenever a neighbor offered us a cool glass of lemonade, or Uncle Eddie handed us the plate of cookies, or a stranger in the grocery store remarked, "Aren't you cute— what a sweet child," our programmed response was always a thank-you. We learned at a young age to use the word "please" to get things, and the words "thank you" to keep these things coming in the future.

Even as adults, if someone holds the door open for us, lets us cut in line at the supermarket because we only have a handful of items, or hands us our order at the drive-through window, we say "Thanks." While saying thanks is important, this act alone does not necessarily indicate thankfulness on the inside, just as expressions like "You're welcome," "How are you doing today?" and "Take care" do not necessarily indicate genuine feeling and concern.

Thankfulness is a state of the heart that directs us to see the beauty that still remains in all situations. To be truly thankful is to continually focus on the ways in which your cup is at least half full. In our culture, this is very difficult. Through advertisements on TV, displays at the mall, the possessions of our neighbors, and the successes of celebrities and public figures, we are constantly bombarded with messages of the scarcity in our own lives. These messages tell us that there is something other people have that we deserve to have but do not yet have, and that we must quickly procure that thing before it is totally gone.

In a society that is far healthier and wealthier than any in recorded history, many of us are plagued by the haunting fear that we are somehow failing to get our fair share. Even when the stock market is bullishly pushing to new heights every week and personal incomes are increasing for many, the proportion of giving to churches and charities tends to drop. Instead of a heart of thankfulness, we have developed a heart of stinginess that focus on the emptiness of our personal cup rather than its fullness. We celebrate Thanksgiving Day with bountiful food and as many people as we can fit around the table, but how many of our hearts are truly thankful on the inside?

President Abraham Lincoln illustrated the essence of a thankful heart when he proclaimed the first Thanksgiving Day in 1863. As a nation, we were in the middle of one of the most divisive and destructive periods of our history—the Civil War. We had already buried thousands of husbands and brothers, and thousands more would lose their lives before hostilities ended. Still, Lincoln saw the need for giving thanks as a nation for our blessings, because he recognized that the nation had existed for many years in peace and prosperity, and had grown in population, wealth, and power as no other nation had ever grown.

Lincoln also wrote in his Thanksgiving Day proclamation about how we as a nation had forgotten the role that God played. "We have forgotten the gracious hand that preserved us in peace and multiplied and enriched and strengthened us," he said, "but instead imagined that these results were produced by some superior wisdom and virtue of our own." Lincoln then indicated his intention to set apart one day a year in which God would be solemnly, reverently, and gratefully acknowledged by the whole American people.

The fruits of a thankful attitude are contentment, self-control, and free acknowledgement of the contributions of others. At home, this attitude can be seen in many ways. My wife recently illustrated it as she was tarrying in bed one morning and heard our daughter and me getting ready for the day. A year earlier, we had purchased an older home and totally remodeled it on the inside. While we were able to redo kitchen and bathrooms and create a new family room down-stairs, we decided to exhibit fiscal restraint and put off installing a carpet runner up the stairs. Consequently, any footsteps on the steps or noises in other parts of the house bounced off hardwood floors and hard plaster walls and were perfectly audible from the upstairs bedrooms. This feature had quickly become an irritant to any of the four of us who sought a quiet place in which to think or sleep.

However, as my wife lay there that morning, the sounds of feet on the floor and cupboards banging took on a whole new per-spective. She was suddenly and profoundly struck by how blessed she was to have this husband and this daughter in her life—as well as our son, who at the time was away at college—and how wonderful it was to actually hear the evidence of us in her life. In that moment, her heart was transformed from one of discontent to one of thankfulness. The actual situation of reverberating noise had not changed, but she had been trans-formed on the inside by her attitude of thankfulness.

This same kind of transformation occurs at work for those who have developed thankful attitudes. For example, Donna was a young manager who had recently joined one of my client companies. The department she took over was in disarray when she arrived, and she began to feverishly work at pulling it together. She was driven to turn around the negative perceptions that the rest of the organization had toward her new group.

While it was apparent to her manager that Donna was highly motivated to make a difference, it also became clear that Donna was entirely too focused on the "half-empty" part of the cup when it came to her department. The harder she worked at turning things around and the longer the hours she logged, the more brittle and defensive her attitude became until she began blowing up in front of others inside and outside of her department.

My coaching with Donna first focused on the self-defeating fears and irrational beliefs that put pressure on her and an edge on her behavior with others. Once we got a handle on why she reacted so strongly to criticism, we began to focus on how she could become more of a wholehearted leader within her department. The breakthrough came as we discussed the element of thankfulness.

Donna identified the many aspects of her life for which she was deeply thankful—particularly her family and the job that allowed her to help her husband support them. Then she began to recognize the many ways she was thankful to her team for how they had risen to the challenges she had placed before them. Finally, she recognized how thankful she was to her boss for being supportive and not putting undue pressure on her to turn things around immediately. This simple shift in thinking made it possible for her to go back to the very same circumstances that had previously existed, but with a new attitude that others found attractive and motivating. She was able to focus only on the beauty that still remained in her work and life.

I found it easy to relate to Donna because in the early 1990s my own vocational situation seemed rather grim. I was spending long hours at a job that offered little in the way of independent thought or creativity, and reporting to people who seemed to have little respect or personal liking for me. It was a miserable several–month stretch as I ruminated on my situation and was unable to envision a way out of it. All I was able to focus on was the misery—the beauty was totally obscured.

One day, however, I began to recognize how my pessimism about work had begun to poison my relationships with my wife and children. Most days I came home exhausted and depressed, irritable and stressed, and my toxic attitude pushed my family away from me. On the day I recognized what I had become, I determined that I would begin to shift my attitude from pessimism to optimism, from resentment to thankfulness, from misery to beauty, and that I would start one day at a time.

On the way home from work the next day, I decided to focus on all the events from the day for which I was thankful. I thought long and hard and came up empty for anything to be thankful about. In fact, the only thing my heart could truly get excited about was that the sky was blue and cloudless on the way home and the sun was still up. Winter in Minnesota was at last turning into spring and the days were getting longer. It was a tenuous beginning, but a start nonetheless on my new thankful attitude.

From that bit of blue sky, I began on successive days and weeks to think about my wife, children, and Max, our golden retriever, who would all be excited about my coming home after work. After a few weeks, I began to recall all the people and events for which I was thankful during a particular day before I returned home to my family. It began to make a noticeable difference in my interactions at home.

My next step was to think about how thankful I was for my family and work on the way to my job. Eventually, I was able to focus on all the people and events I was actually looking forward to that day as I drove into work in the morning. After a short while of sandwiching my day with a thick slice of thankfulness in the morning and another slice of thankfulness in the evening, my attitude made a permanent shift. Though I still got frustrated with people and situations at my place of employment, my overall sense of thankfulness helped me to quickly get over these.

Over the years, I have asked participants to share in workshop groups what they are thankful for in their lives. These are typical responses I have received:

- Family—spouse, children, grandchildren
- Friends, other people in my life, special mentors
- Good company to work for, good job with great coworkers, being employed
- My talents, sense of humor, peace of mind, ability to focus on the present
- Positive role models, my roots, experiences while growing up
- Having a home, decent place to live, financial security, food to eat
- Belief in God, relationship to God
- Pets
- Good health—mental and physical
- To be alive, to be living at this time in the world, living in a free country
- The accomplishment of my goals
- Good education, knowledge

- People from the past who have made us who we are
- Things that make me laugh

Wholehearted Thankfulness

Jim Warner calls the beauty that remains a matter of perspective, and explains that in the United States today—our fears of terrorism not withstanding—it is almost absurd not to be thankful. Unfortunately, most Americans are isolated from the real poverty, hopelessness, and trapped feelings that people living in other less wealthy countries experience. Jim's wife and friends help him keep a thankful perspective by reminding him of his many blessings in his life. He takes the old expression "count your blessings" literally and makes it real and alive by reviewing the many positives about his health, family, opportunities, and possessions on a daily basis.

Each day, Jim recites out loud what he is thankful for, focuses for a moment on each of these, then thinks about the aspects of his life that he is committed to change. Because of this focus on the blessings in his life, Jim is able to live each day with the belief that "my cup is 95 percent full," and to know that he can handle the other 5 percent without getting emotionally distraught. According to Jim, "thankfulness is not a spontaneous, uncontrollable feeling, but a mental process—a decision I can make each day to be thankful."

Chuck Slocum believes that finding the beauty that remains and developing a sense of thankfulness is a very spiritual undertaking. "By focusing on your assets as well as the people you love, it's not a giant leap to feel a sense of thankfulness for it all," he believes. "Even with large financial pressures like supporting kids in college or spouses losing their jobs, we ought to be in constant conversation with God about how thankful we are for his provision in our lives. I'm just so grateful to have a life partner—my wife—who is so special to me. I'm also grateful for who I am and for the faith that the Lord will continue to provide for my needs."

Trudy Canine has learned a great deal about the power of thankfulness just in the last year or so. When not running her small business or shuttling her two sons around to their various school and extracurricular activities, Trudy provides mentoring for a middle school girl who has struggled with acting out and getting into trouble. The young girl was trying hard to turn herself around, but already had such a negative reputation that she felt all her efforts to change were futile.

In the midst of the girl's discouragement, Trudy was spontaneously moved to suggest that together they make a list of "everything that's good about you." As the list grew—dancer, basketball player, bright and articulate person, good friend— the girl's face began to brighten and her energy perked up. Trudy suggested that she continue to build on the list to remind herself of these aspects of herself and her life for which she was truly thankful.

And when others said or appeared to be thinking negative, defeating things about her, Trudy suggested she respond by saying, "It's easy to see all the things that are wrong with me. Let's talk about the things that are right with me." At last report, the young woman—armed with these thankfulness strategies and the help of others in her environment besides Trudy—was making a dramatic turnaround both at home and at school.

Trudy also tells the story of how one of her outplacement clients taught her some important lessons about the power of appreciation. After every one of their sessions, this client sent Trudy an e-mail message in which she expressed her appreciation for every specific part of the interaction that was helpful to her. "She was totally focused on the positives, and I was inspired to do even more for her," recalls Trudy. "It set an incredible foundation for our subsequent meetings. I learned how important this is for growing and sustaining relationships—just telling people what I appreciate about them!" Trudy suggests that such expressions of appreciation are most effective when they are sincere, connected to specific actions of the other person, and focused on what the interaction meant to you—how you grew as a result of the experience.

Dave and Carol Graff run their own marketing research business, Graff Group, from two separate offices in their home. They help corporate clients gather market and customer information, as well as create marketing strategies. Carol indicated that being married and working a home-based business together can create a very difficult environment. "It can be lonely and stressful at times, and can challenge your relationship," she said. Dave finds it more difficult than does Carol to draw boundaries between work and personal life, especially now that they are empty nesters. They both do what they can to create some healthy boundaries—like taking a class without the other, finding friends that the other does not share, or just getting out of the home office for a breather.

Despite daily challenges, however, the Graffs focus on the beauty that remains and have developed a strong sense of thankfulness. They are very aware that their clients have choices of who to use in the marketplace, so that when the clients decide to use Graff Group for their business, Dave and Carol are truly thankful. "We thank God and our client for their business, and we always send a handwritten, personal note with each invoice," explains Dave, "because we recognize that without them, we wouldn't be in business." Carol adds, "The current business environment and economy is very challenging and because of the significant uncertainty, our clients are often stressed. The more we can affirm—even in small ways—what's going right in their lives, the more we can make a difference for them. When you really connect with your clients, you can easily find something to say from the heart."

Every year at Thanksgiving time, the Graffs send out a special message of thanks to their clients. They try to make the form of the message creative and as memorable as possible, while at the same time sending a sincere, thankful communication that is from the heart. Every year at this time, Dave and Carol also make a donation to the Salvation Army in the name of their clients. "We have a lot to be thankful for and we want to make it crystal clear to our clients that we appreciate and are honored by their trust in us," says Dave.

Earlier in this chapter, I described my own shift toward thankfulness. My suggestion to you is to try the prescription of "one thankfulness sandwich every day" until the pessimism is gone, and then on an as-needed basis after that. Develop a habit of starting off every day or each interaction during the day with thanks in your heart for all the ways in which you have been blessed in your life. Then end each day or each interaction with thanks for how things went. In this way, it is possible to wrap each part of each day in a spirit of thankfulness that generates energy and enthusiasm for the next part of the day—all day long. Pretty soon, all you will notice is the beauty that still remains.

As we have seen, focusing on the good things and being thankful does not change your circumstances one bit, but it alters the attitude with which you view and interact with those circumstances. If you want a wonderful family and great friends, start by thinking about how thankful you are for them. Then tell them, pray for them, demonstrate to them your love and gratitude. If you long to have a job where you love the company and your coworkers, start by focusing on the ways in which you are thankful for them. Then begin to show and tell them how appreciative you are. Start by believing and acting as if people around you are worthy of your thanks, then notice how your positive attitude affects their behavior.

When things are bad, we take comfort in the thought that they could always be worse. And when they are, we find hope in the thought that things are so bad they have to get better.

—*Malcolm S. Forbes*

5 | FIND HOPE IN THE THOUGHT THAT THINGS WILL GET BETTER

The core difference between an optimist and a pessimist is that the former digs down inside and finds hope that tomorrow will dawn as a new day and things will be better with a fresh start. According to *Webster's Third New International Dictionary*, "optimism" comes from Latin through French and originates from the word "optimum", or "that which is best." The French word *optimisme* was in fact used to describe the doctrine of Liebniz, a noted philosopher who believed that this world is the best possible world in which we could anticipate the best possible results because it was created by an all-wise, all-powerful, and all-good God.

In more current parlance, the word "optimism" has come to mean an attitude in which a person views events from the most positive perspective and anticipates the best possible outcomes—the hope that things will get better. This hope or optimism, then, is based on the trust that one's needs and desires will continue to be met. There is an important distinction between hope and "Pollyannaism." Optimists are able to look at any situation with clear awareness of the potential dangers but choose instead to focus on the potential opportunities. Those with a Pollyanna attitude focus on the upside potential without ever considering the downside. Hope, then, is a choice to focus on the positive in the midst of an awareness of the negative.

Our history is filled with stories of leaders who exhibited optimism in all fields of endeavor. The biblical event of David, the young Hebrew shepherd boy, confidently facing Goliath, the giant Philistine warrior, is a classic story of optimism on the part of both of these combatants. Examples from the more recent past include Colonel Sanders, who spent days driving from restaurant to café (and nights sleeping in the back seat of his car) trying to convince the skeptical owners to use his new Kentucky Fried Chicken recipe. Or Thomas Edison, who labored day after day, month after month, trying out thousands of filaments until he found the one that successfully carried an electrical current through a glass bulb to create illumination.

Hope and optimism are closely related to faith. All three are founded on beliefs that create an enthusiastic, wholehearted attitude within the individual. Leaders who are infused with optimism, faith, and hope put their primary focus on the "half-full" aspects of the cup in front of them. They have keen awareness of the "half-empty" potential, but choose instead to generate vision and energy around the upside.

Focusing on the upside does not mean that you sit back and wait for someone else to meet your needs, but rather that you actively engage in work, expecting the best results. From optimism springs the faith that things will work out, negative phases will pass, situations will develop positively, and problems will be resolved in a win–win manner. Without optimism, discouragement, worry, and overwhelmed feelings can prevail.

Nobody and no situation has the power to create your attitude—only you do. No matter what the circumstances around you, no one can force you to adopt a pessimistic attitude. In all situations, you have the power to choose your attitude. An optimistic attitude is a conscious choice you can make, and it has a tremendous impact on how well things actually do work out and the extent to which you find a silver lining in the dark clouds.

As a society, we have been from the early years a culture of hope. Optimistic explorers looking for a shortcut to the Far East first landed on American soil; they were soon followed by hopeful religious reformers looking for a place where they could live their beliefs without repression. Later settlers were optimistic about making a living or finding a fortune that was denied them for one reason or another in the country of their birth. Perhaps they were not the first-born son and thus had no inheritance, or perhaps they were from a poor and down-trodden family. America represented a fresh opportunity, an optimistic chance to support themselves and their families in a land with unlimited upside potential.

Throughout our history as a nation, the sports world has been filled with examples of optimism that cross age, race, and sex. Muhammad Ali told the world that he was the greatest, then commenced to prove it over and over in the boxing ring. Babe Ruth optimistically pointed to the left field bleachers, signaling the direction of his home run ball even though statistics showed that he struck out three times as often as he homered. Wilma Rudolph overcame a crippling childhood disease to become a world-class and world-renowned runner in the Olympic sprint events. More recently, Lance Armstrong overcame cancer to win the Tour de France—four times and counting.

Where does this hope come from? The optimism of these people and others is based on faith. To have faith is to have a firm belief in some outcome for which there is little or no evidence. Everyone has faith in something or someone and that faith can either be positive—"it will work out, I will be successful"—or negative—"it never works out for me, someone always takes advantage of me." Positive faith is what I call optimism.

Faith is always attached to someone or something. People tend to put their faith in a combination of four places: themselves, other people, technology/methodology, or a higher power. Your degree of optimism stems from the level of faith you have in one or more of these sources.

Let's look at some familiar situations to illustrate these various objects of faith. Some people who invest in the stock market seem to have faith or trust in themselves. That is, they do their own research and make their own investments. Others seem to trust in investment brokers who manage the funds for them. People who drive fast on foggy or icy roads seem to have faith in themselves and their ability behind the wheel. They might also trust that other drivers will not suddenly pull out in front of them and lose control, and might have faith in the technology of their own vehicles to handle it. People who make major life decisions by first praying to God, reading their horoscope, or consulting a psychic are putting their faith in a power they assume to be higher than their own. In the David and Goliath account cited earlier, Goliath had faith in himself and his armaments, while David put his faith in his God.

The amount of faith in ourselves, other people, technology/methodology, or a higher power is directly proportional to how much we know about the object of our faith. People will reveal this with words such as, "I have a lot of confidence in myself," or "Sally is trustworthy, I know I can count on her to live up to her word." Over time, the evidence is generated in our own results or in the consistency of people, and our faith either grows or diminishes.

People such as actor Christopher Reeve represent those who have a great deal of faith in technology. Reeve, best known for his movie roles as Superman, became paralyzed from the neck down after a jumping accident while riding his horse. He has expressed the confidence that spinal cord medical technology will develop at a fast enough pace that he will walk again in his lifetime. As he becomes more knowledgeable about his injuries and the medical breakthroughs related to it, he will become more or less optimistic about the object of this faith—technology.

The curve of faith development typically goes like this:
- increasing faith as you learn more about the object of your faith
- leveling off as you begin to assess the effectiveness of the path you have chosen
- increasing or decreasing faith depending on how you perceive the process and results

Faith is also an action word. That is, if you truly have faith in yourself, others, technology/methodology, or a higher power, then you will act according to that faith. I have coached a number of corporate executives and managers who say they have faith in themselves but then hesitate to step forward or to make the decisions that must be made. Others express their trust in me as a coach and in the confidentiality of our work together, but then hold back critical issues and information from our coaching sessions. It is not difficult to see by people's actions how much faith they actually have.

As we have seen, optimism is the belief that our needs will continue to be met, that things will work out for the best in our lives. While to a certain extent we can buttress our faith by looking backward for an evidential trend line, the degree of our faith mostly depends on the object in which we believe, how much we know about the object, and the extent to which we put our beliefs into action.

You have probably recognized that being around an optimist is much more fun than hanging out with a pessimist. Optimists not only tend to see the positive in people and situations, they also are more likely to be generous with their time, energy, and money. They are more likely to view their resources as bottomless springs that will get replenished somehow. From these observations, we can probably conclude that optimists have more friends and more fun in life. There is also strong scientific evidence that optimism has very tangible and positive health benefits.

A recent report from the Mayo Clinic in Rochester, Minnesota, described the results of a longitudinal study of more than 800 individuals who, 35 years earlier, had answered a set of questions. The questions, pulled from the Minnesota Multiphasic Personality Inventory (MMPI), assessed the extent to which respondents' attitudes were optimistic, pessimistic, or somewhere in the middle. The results indicated that the most optimistic among them tended to live significantly longer than the most pessimistic, regardless of age or sex, and had fewer mental and physical health issues. Other research has shown that pessimists develop weaker immune systems, are more prone to colds and flu, and experience more major health problems after age 50.

In a recent workshop, a participant described what he believed to be his own optimistic attitude. He told the group, "If I think something will really turn out well, I prepare myself for the worst so I won't be disappointed in the end. Usually, I tell myself that things won't turn out well so that if instead they do turn out well, then I'm happily surprised rather than disappointed." I thanked him for his perspective and then gently explained why I thought this "optimism" that he just illustrated was really a pessimistic attitude covered over with a positive veneer.

If we truly are hopefully optimistic in our attitudes, we do not need to prepare ourselves for the worst, but rather prepare ourselves for the best. Henry Ford said that whether people believe they can do something or not, either way they are right. If we believe we can do something, we usually can; if we believe we cannot accomplish a task, we typically cannot.

An optimist recognizes the possibility of a negative outcome, but chooses to focus on the probability of a positive outcome, and puts all of her energies toward that goal. My own experience tells me that I am more likely to achieve a positive result if I approach the situation with an optimistic attitude. While choosing a pessimistic attitude might seem like a good way to protect yourself from disappointment, it typically does not lead to an optimistic result.

The Optimism of Wholehearted Leaders

Meghan Brown, director of human resources for TAPE-MARK Company, is a perfect example of someone who was able to consciously shift her attitude from one of dark pessimism to one of continuous optimism. In the past, Meghan has experienced the weight of depression and concluded that she must either rid her mind of the negative thoughts or decide to be unhappy forever. This is the process she uses to keep an optimistic focus:

- Catch yourself having discouraging, unhealthy thoughts, like "this won't work, you're not good enough, you're the victim here"
- Recognize that continuing to have these thoughts will lead you down "the dark steps" where you have been before
- Realize that pessimism is the "energy zapper" and that negative thinking only leads to where there is no energy to change the situation

- Determine that you will use all the energy you have each day to focus on positive thoughts and feelings, and create optimistic outcomes

It takes a great deal of diligence to catch yourself every time negative thoughts come up and then use the steps described above to shift to positive thoughts and feelings. Meghan uses humor to help her shift her beliefs toward optimism. Crediting her parents for modeling the use of humor to get through tough situations, she has developed the capacity to laugh about things that in the past would have discouraged her.

How does she know that she is not just heavily in denial when bad things happen? Meghan believes that if her hope was not genuine, it would take so much energy to keep up the front that it would lead eventually to a depressive reaction. She credits her faith in God for the power to maintain hope and optimism in the face of negative situations that arise at work and at home.

Jim Warner notes that continuing to be optimistic in any circumstance in which he finds himself is the challenge. He defines optimism as "a commitment to being positive, no matter the circumstances." It is easy to be optimistic when things are going well, but true optimists continue to be thankful and positive when things are not going well. They trust that all situations eventually will work out to a positive outcome.

Optimists take the long view in which they recognize that they might not be able to actually see the positive outcome from their present vantage point, but may only see it in hindsight from much further down the road.

Illustrating this approach, Jim describes a technique in which he maintains his optimistic attitude by living his life today in the context of his life up to this point. When something happens that is discouraging or frustrating, he thinks back to other times when he felt pessimistic and reminds himself that most of these situations have turned out very positively. This helps to reduce the impact of pessimistic, irrational fears. Jim typically calms himself and provides perspective by telling himself, "it's worked out in the past and it will most likely work out in the future."

Jim developed this hopeful attitude in spite of several situations in his life that would have discouraged most people. He confides that early in his life he had a sizable investment and then lost it all. At the time it felt like he would never recover from this financial disaster. In short order, however, he was able to regain his optimistic perspective by asking how important was the money in his life and remembering what he still had that was of greater value—his significant relationships.

Jim also exhibited great optimism about having a loving family as he stayed single until age 40, patiently waiting for the right woman to enter his life. He met and fell in love with Cheryl; when they married he was blessed with an instant family because she already had three daughters from a previous marriage. The blessings continued—since their marriage in 1991, Jim and Cheryl have adopted two more daughters.

Trudy Canine's hopefulness involves "taking an appreciative stance—finding things to appreciate in what is before me." What is before her might include her family, coworkers, colleagues or clients in her field, or others from her community. "I try to think in terms of what I want more of—not thinking, for example, 'they're too crabby,' but instead thinking, 'I wish they were in a better humor.' I try to pay attention to what I want to grow in my life and focus on this preferred future rather than on the aspects that are wrong in my current reality."

When she recently lost in a bid for the mayoral race in her home town, it was the hardest thing she had ever faced because it was the first major event in her life that didn't have a successful outcome. During the race for mayor, she had a strong faith that God was with her and that all she needed to do was to listen for his guidance. When she lost the race, it was very painful at first, but then she began to see that perhaps God wanted her to learn something about loss. "It became very clear to me how losses can end up being the best lessons in life," Trudy noted.

Describing himself as an optimistic person, Barry Brottlund credits his lack of pessimistic thought patterns to his parents who have been encouraging and confidence-building throughout his life. "I have never felt like everything was doom and gloom even when all my circumstances were over-whelmingly negative," he said.

Barry also calls upon his faith to maintain a positive attitude day to day, stating, "I know I'm here for a purpose. Everything that happens to me, no matter how hopeless, pointless, or insignificant it might seem, has an ultimate positive purpose in God's eyes. My daily prayer is to be open and ready to recognize what that purpose might be. I can go back in my life and identify the worst situations I went through—including divorce and financial disaster—and now see the positive purpose in each of them."

As Meghan, Barry, Trudy, and Jim illustrate, optimism is a learned attitude that can be developed or decreased. Pessimism is also a learned attitude. These four report, as you might expect, that they are not always optimistic. They have learned some pessimism along the way and must work hard to unlearn it. Jim confides that there have been and continue to be times when the circumstances feel overwhelming, very real and very painful. At times like these, he slips back into unthankfulness, resentment, and discouragement—some of the learned attitudes of pessimism from earlier in his life. "No matter who you are, you have your line to walk to stay on the optimistic side," he notes.

Shifting your Attitude to Optimism

The process of shifting your attitude to optimism involves three steps:

1. recognizing the pessimism in your attitude
2. consciously deciding to change your beliefs, and then
3. behaving consistently according to your new optimistic beliefs

We will take a closer look at each of these three steps to becoming more consistently optimistic in your life.

Recognizing the pessimism in your own attitude is arguably the most difficult step of the three. It requires that you pull back from your own behaviors and get perspective on them. This is hard for most people to do on their own. Even with the help of a spouse or trusted friend, expecting them to be comfortable enough to gently confront you with your pessimism can be like expecting them to tell you when you have bad breath. The honest feedback of colleagues on a 360-

degree, multi-rater feedback form can help to illuminate critical, abrasive, or discouraging behaviors that might indicate the existence of pessimistic beliefs below the surface. No matter how you achieve perspective on your pessimism, the key is that you recognize it and take responsibility for its existence without blaming it on another person or situation in your life.

Once the pessimism is recognized as a problem, the next step is the conscious decision to change your beliefs. This conscious choice requires you to be convinced of the importance of an optimistic attitude in the various roles you play in your life and to be committed to creating a fundamental change in this area.

One approach to changing to a more optimistic attitude is to dig deeply to develop insight about where the pessimistic beliefs may have originated. A likely place to start is to identify the faulty beliefs that get in the way of your peak performance and then choose to change those beliefs to more optimistic ones. It is a matter of shifting your heart and your mind and committing to replace pessimism with a continually growing optimism.

Dick, owner of a home-based financial services business, illustrated this shift in thinking when he purposely created a long list of his pessimistic beliefs and countered them on the other side of the page with optimistic beliefs. His list looked like this:

Pessimistic/faulty	*Optimistic/accurate*
• Avoiding failure leads to success	• Success comes with risk & learning from failures
• If you can't do it perfectly, don't do it at all	• "Perfectly adequate" is O.K.
• If you can't deal with a problem, just put it off until it resolves itself	• Problems are easier to fix if handled right away
• I don't have all the information, so I can't make a decision	• I have enough information to decide right now
• I won't look stupid if I just keep quiet	• Smart people are the ones who have ideas, contribute them, and ask questions

Another approach to creating optimism is to focus on the direction you want to go rather than on the problems and obstacles from your past. By first creating a hopeful vision and then generating ideas about ways to reach that vision, you can focus on the possibilities and, in the process, handle the problems. A good way to start this "hopeful conversation" is to think of times when you have experienced the kind of excitement, energy, and joy that you want to have as a part of your future vision. Reminding yourself or telling others stories of these peak experiences is a great way to kick off a hopeful conversation. Stories are powerful learning strategies because they are based on what you have actually experienced, not just on what you learned in books or seminars.

Once you have reminded yourself of experiences or shared your stories with others, you can begin to look for common themes in the stories. You can identify, for example, underlying values, beliefs, and other elements that existed in each of the stories you shared that you would like to re–create in your future vision. Pulling together the common themes can give you a structure for achieving your new vision. After you have framed out the structure of your vision with the foundation of these values and beliefs, you can begin to look at the gap between where you are now and where you want to be. In the analysis of this gap, you will begin to address the obstacles to your vision.

We have looked at a couple of approaches to creating an optimistic attitude in ourselves and others. The final step in living with an optimistic attitude is to behave in a way that is consistent with our new, optimistic beliefs. In this step, it is helpful to enlist the aid of a spouse, or friends, family members, and coworkers to create consistency in your new behavior.

I experienced this in my own family around the issue of sarcasm. For me—and also for my son whom I inadvertently influenced—sarcasm was considered a highly esteemed form of humor. What I was blind to, however, was that others around me—particularly my wife and daughter—did not find my sarcasm to be humorous at all. In fact, they experienced it as critical and attacking.

Once I recognized the negative element of sarcasm and decided to change this behavior, the next step was to delete it from my repertoire. After more than four decades of practice, this was not as easy as it seemed it should be, so I enlisted the help of my wife and daughter. We imagined what our family would look like and how we would relate without sarcasm. We identified behaviors that would be included in sarcasm. The rest of my family became affectionately referred to as the "sarcasm police," and they were relatively merciless in confronting my use of it. After several months of consistent policing, my sarcasm was nearly extinct and I had become so good at stopping it that I began to amuse myself by catching my wife and daughter on the rare occasions they would emit sarcastic comments.

Taking a more hopeful path begins with recognizing the ways in which you are functioning pessimistically and ends with taking deliberate actions to nurture your optimistic side. When travelling this path of hope, it becomes easier and easier to believe that your needs and desires will continue to be met, regardless of the circumstances around you. As you look back at negative experiences in your life, you begin to see the beauty—the positive purpose and outcome to each. Each time you do this, you take a step closer to becoming the wholehearted leader you were intended to be.

Do whatever comes your way as well as you can. Think as little as possible about yourself and as much as possible about other people.

—*Eleanor Roosevelt*

6 | THINK LESS ABOUT YOURSELF AND MORE ABOUT OTHERS

This vital truth is based on the belief that you will be most effective in your various life roles if you focus your attention right now on helping others around you to be successful. There are two critical aspects in this belief. The first is that your focus must be in the present moment, not looking backward at the past or facing forward toward the future. While there are times when your focus needs to be on memories from the past or on visions of the future, too many of us eat up valuable present time regretting and resenting past events and people encountered, or worrying about disastrous future possibilities.

Too much of a negative focus on the past or the future can lead to an inability to effectively handle issues of the present. The best advice I have ever found on this topic comes from the gospel of Matthew, quoting Jesus (Matthew 6:25 and 6:34, *Holy Bible, New International Version*):

> Therefore I tell you, do not worry about your life, what you will eat or drink; or about your body, what you will wear. Is not life more important than food, and the body more important than clothes?. Therefore, do not worry about tomorrow, for

tomorrow will worry about itself. Each day has enough trouble of its own.

In saying that each day has enough trouble of its own, Jesus seems also to be directing us not to ruminate about yesterday or worry about tomorrow. By instructing us not to worry about our lives, he is instructing us to focus our attention on the lives of others. This is a critically important element of wholehearted leadership and one that our popular culture does little to support.

If, like me, you grew up in the 1960s and '70s, you are well aware of the popular cultural messages to "Do your own thing," "Look out for number one," and "Have it your way." These and hundreds of other messages bombarding our culture in the last 30 years have served to turn our attention mostly toward ourselves and our needs. Ironically, the more we have turned our attention to fulfilling our own needs and desires and the more stuff that we have acquired as a society, the less satisfied we seem to be with our lives! For many people, this focus on themselves has resulted in a life that is simply out of focus. They have been caught in the trap of thinking more about themselves and less about others.

Unfortunately, I did not become fully aware of the power of focusing on others until I was in my late thirties. After attending several self-development workshops, I became aware of the power that fear played in my life and how difficult it was for me to get past that fear in order to truly focus on the needs of others. I later recognized that my primary fear is personal rejection. At the time, I was working as an outplacement consultant helping individuals get refocused so they could decide what they wanted to do in their careers and lives. I still remember times I would walk out to the waiting room to pick up my next appointment and anxiously wonder, "How the heck am I going to be able to help this person?"

But I also vividly remember the morning after my newly gained perspective on fear when for the first time I truly focused on the guy waiting for me in the lobby. He looked very frightened—uncomfortable with his new role as job seeker—and tried desperately to project a confident, somewhat condescending demeanor to other job seekers sitting around him. My focus had shifted sufficiently from me and my own fears and inadequacies to this other person, and suddenly I could truly see him. What followed was the most powerful coaching session I had conducted up to that point.

A year later, I was standing in front of a group preparing to introduce myself when I became acutely aware of how my fear of their rejection and my own self-focused drives caused me to try very hard to be funny and clever. I was struck by how much my focus was always on me—wondering whether or not people liked me. What followed over the next months and years was a gradual process of catching myself focusing on my own needs while I was speaking or listening, and then shifting that focus toward what the person or group of people were telling me they needed. I began to powerfully attend to their nonverbal behaviors and the feelings behind their questions and comments.

My presentations and workshops became less of a performance and more of an intimate conversation. By truly focusing on my audience of one or many, I was able to give them what they needed most. In the past several years, I have continued to discover how much more effective I am in my work when I place my focus primarily on others. I have also learned how to let go of my own agenda and to let God powerfully work through me as I coach and train leaders.

The first part of focusing primarily on the needs of others, then, is to create that focus right now, this moment—without worrying about the past or the future. The second part is to take your focus off of you and your needs and place your attention primarily on the needs of others around you—your family, customers, friends, neighbors, and coworkers. In focusing on others, ask yourself what you can do to make them more effective and successful in their endeavors. Set aside your own agenda and to-do list in order to give others the attention they need right now.

Focusing on others requires us to get past our own self-focused drives and irrational fears. Once past these obstacles, attending to others requires an approach that keeps us focused on them and clearly communicates this focus to them. Your focused approach, then, must begin with some nonverbal, internal components.

The Other-Focus of Wholehearted Leaders

Winston Churchill once said that we make a living by what we get, but we make a life by what we give. My former coworker Jim Warner exemplifies the kind of focus Churchill refers to. With the exception of when he is sleeping and getting cleaned up in the morning, Jim's entire 24–hour–day seems to be focused on the needs of others right now. At home, he and his wife Cheryl provide love and shelter for five adopted daughters and occasional foster children who range in age from 3 to 19. The older daughters are active in school and church activities and often need transportation. The younger daughters need laps to sit on and someone to read a book or watch a video with them. A couple of the daughters have medical needs that require extra time and doctor visits.

At work Jim wears three distinct hats. He is in charge of all the administrative support—facilities, programs, expansion of building—and he is the pastoral coach for a church staff of nearly 70, including five other pastors. In addition, he directs the strategic planning for this missions-oriented and rapidly growing church of more than 3,000 members. He and his family have taken several mission trips to Jamaica, one of which led to the adoption of their fifth daughter.

People who know Jim clearly describe him as someone who does not generally ruminate about the past or worry about the future. More important, they describe him as a person who listens to others, attends to their needs, and genuinely cares about them. In short, others recognize that his focus is primarily on *them* when they interact with him—whether it is his wife and daughters, the pastors he shepherds, or the other people at his church. Jim focuses on them because he truly believes that his life will be most successful if their lives are successful, and this belief generates his behaviors.

Rob Stevenson talks about focusing more on others and less on himself in terms of getting rid of the distractions. To that end, he spends a long weekend every year in the silence and solitary reflection of a Jesuit retreat center. At such a retreat, one is able to spend full days with limited distractions (no maintenance tasks such as preparing and cleaning up from meals) and total focus on prayer and meditation. Though some may come away from such a weekend with a greater focus on self, Rob finds that the retreats help him become more disciplined about thoughts and activities that typically distract him from truly focusing on the needs of others in his work and life.

Barry Brottlund describes how he discovered the power of focusing on others when his father passed away in 1995. At the funeral, dozens of people that he did not know came to tell him and his family about what a powerful influence his father had been in their lives. Barry was so moved by these expressions of gratitude that he was determined to understand why his father had so profoundly affected others. He concluded that his father had been "a humble man who spoke the truth and was always encouraging."

Resolved to become like his father in this way, Barry began to truly focus on the needs of others in his work and life. He discovered that a combination of humility and transparency—the capacity to admit mistakes and laugh at himself—were the qualities he saw in his father and most admired in others. "It's an attitude to strive toward," he explained, "and as you develop this attitude, it's amazing how positively people respond to you, because they know they can trust what they see."

"The key for me is being curious," says Trudy Canine. "If I'm always focused on being curious, I will always be asking people about themselves—and they like to tell their stories. My perspective is that people are 'multi-storied' and we get to choose to focus on the wonderful stories about people that are always there to be discovered. You get invited into their world and learn their stories by asking the right questions. As you listen and learn, the magic that happens is that you end up building a lasting, bonding relationship." By being curious and asking open-ended questions that expand the conversation, Trudy has come to realize that sometimes what she thinks is happening in a dialogue is not at all how the other person perceives it. In the exchange of talking about what happened in the conversation for her and the other person, they both can come to a much deeper understanding and a more trusting relationship.

As Jim, Trudy, Barry, and Rob exemplify, the less self-focused your attitude, the more effective you will be with others in your work and life. Focusing on your own needs when working with and relating to others drains your patience, gentleness, kindness, and compassion. Without a focus on others, you are more likely to be frustrated in seeking results, protective of your turf, fearful of others' motives, and distrusted by them.

Strategies for Focusing on Others

Let's look closer at how to think more about others and less about you. First, clear your head of any competing thoughts and questions so that you can focus on the person or group. Make sure you are in an environment with minimal distractions or interruptions that might take your focus away from others. Create an attitude in yourself that is win-win, compassionate, and interested about the person(s) with whom you are communicating. Then, make sure your body is turned toward the person(s) and make clear and steady eye contact. These actions all convey the message that your attention is focused.

Next, open up communication by using some questions or making an observation. Examples of questions include, "How is the project going?" or "What do you think we should do in this situation?" Using openers like "how" and "what" usually encourages people to talk further and opens up the conversation, as compared with questions such as "Is this the best we can expect?" which can be answered with a yes or no response. Instead of questions, you can use statements that encourage communication—"Describe for me what happened yesterday," "Tell me more about the status of the project," or "Help me understand your perspective."

You can also use observations to pick up on feelings that appear to be present in the person or group. Statements such as, "You seem rather upset after what I just said," or "You got quiet suddenly, so I'm wondering how you are reacting to my question?" can be useful in surfacing strong feelings that otherwise might block the conversation. Remember that the objective here is to open up communication and encourage the other person(s) to speak freely.

Once the conversation is off the ground and beginning to fly, you can continue to use open-ended questions and observations to expand the dialogue. Or you can paraphrase or use reflection and summary statements to broaden and deepen the communication. To paraphrase is to summarize a small portion of a conversation so that you are sure you heard it correctly and so that the other person knows you are listening. Reflection is the technique of giving a name to the feelings you perceive in the other person(s) and speaking it out loud to test your hypothesis. The statements below provides examples of both of these methods for expanding a conversation.

> *Person:* This day has been awful! Two customers called to complain about our service, my manager is concerned about some expenses, and a late meeting that just got scheduled conflicts with my daughter's soccer game after school. I'm so frustrated about all the competing demands on me that I can't seem to satisfy.

> *Paraphrase:* Sounds like this has been a hard day for you so far! Between customers, your boss, and your daughter, your day is way too complicated.

> *Reflection:* Ouch! Your day seems overwhelming and frustrating. You've got people pushing on all sides and are worried you won't be able to pull it together enough to satisfy any of them!

Following several such exchanges over a number of minutes, you can employ a summary statement to expand the communication. Summary statements occur less often than paraphrasing and reflection, and are used to provide a temporary pause in a conversation to make sure you are still tracking each other. Think of summary statements as an extended paraphrase that gives the speakers a moment to pause and regroup for the next phase.

When you want to bring the conversation to a close, do so with a gentle statement such as, "It has been great to have a chance to talk and catch up on your day. I need to head off to a meeting right now, so we'll need to bring this to a close." You simply comment on the dialogue, then indicate your need to bring it to a close. If that seems too abrupt because of the nature of your conversation up that point, you can also close it in an open-ended way such as, "Thanks for sharing with me what's been happening in your day. I need to go to my next appointment right now, but we could talk again later today or during the week. Which would be best for you?" This statement asserts your need to end the conversation now, but clearly provides an opening to continue it later.

I am convinced that this belief in the importance of focusing primarily on others in all interpersonal interactions is the key to any leader's effectiveness. An old expression says that there is a good reason God gave people two ears and two eyes—but only one mouth! He intended for us to be watching and listening more than speaking. Focusing on others means listening to them with both your ears and your eyes and truly understanding them before expressing your own needs and thoughts.

Hearty laughter is a good way to jog internally without having to go outdoors.

—*Norman Cousins*

7 | JOG YOURSELF PHYSICALLY, PSYCHOLOGICALLY, SPIRITUALLY

Of all the creatures on the face of the earth, human beings appear to be unique in their need for refreshment that is physical, psychological, and spiritual. Though I am no expert in the area of animals, I have watched enough hours of *Animal Planet* and other television shows with my teenaged daughter, Kate, to have seen no evidence of creatures with spiritual needs. I have, however, observed animals needing sleep, food, cool shade, and rest. I have also observed them needing to play-fight, chase an object, shake or knock around a ball or stuffed animal, and get various parts of their bodies scratched or stroked. These examples would appear to indicate that animals have the need to refresh themselves both physically and psychologically.

Only with human beings, however, have I observed the need for physical, psychological, and spiritual refreshment. From the physical perspective, we human beings need to sleep and eat meals every day, to exercise and stretch, and to rest or pace ourselves with physical labor. From the psychological perspective, we require activities that interest us, entertainment that captures our attention, love and respect from others, and the opportunity to play. These two sets of needs are not all that different from many species of animals.

As human beings, however, we also have the need to be refreshed spiritually. Though this is unique to humans, not all humans recognize this facet of themselves. One individual I coached recently looked at me blankly when I started talking about these three areas of human need for refreshment, and said, "I don't really have a spiritual side."

I explained to him that all human beings have a spiritual side, but that for many people that side is unexplored and foreign. Then I described to him what I meant by the word "spiritual." I indicated to him that on the most fundamental level human beings have a need to connect with something or someone that is bigger and more powerful than they are. It is simply the way humans are built, and it is very different from the other animals. I have heard people describe this need as the "God-shaped hole" that all people have in their hearts.

We human beings are unique, then, in our need for refreshment in all three of the physical, psychological, and spiritual areas. I believe that refreshment in these areas is more effective if it is done on a regular daily or weekly basis rather than in large sporadic doses.

You can readily convince yourself of the truth of this last statement by thinking about the last time you and your family went on that two-week annual vacation. For a week or two before the start of the vacation, you probably worked extra hours with extra intensity at your job to make sure everything was handled before you left. You woke your family up at 4 A.M. to get to the airport in time to make that 7 A.M. flight. When you arrived at the airport, you discovered that your flight had been delayed due to mechanical problems. Eventually the flight was cancelled, but you managed to get on a later flight with your family spread out in single seats over the entire aircraft. By the time this plane landed, you had missed your connecting flight but got on a later one and arrived at your destination by midnight. Unfortunately, your bags were misrouted and were not there to greet you, but you managed to get the family safely to the hotel and tucked in bed by 2 A.M.

For the first several days of the vacation, you had trouble relaxing and continued to be bothered by worries about what you forgot to finish at work, what was not turned off at home, and why your kids forgot to pack their favorite shampoo and half their clothes. By the end of the first week, you began to really relax and not think about anything but the family and vacation fun.

However, about three days before the end of your stay, you began to get irritable and short with the kids and your spouse. You started to think about work and all the e—mail and voice mail messages, memos, and issues that would be there upon your return. You began to make plans to go into work on the Sunday night when you get back in town so that Monday morning would not be so stressful. Two days before your return, you broke down and checked your voice mail from the hotel phone and discovered that one of your subordinates had made a major blunder with your best client.

You get the idea. The vital truth about refreshment is that it is critical to build in physical, psychological, spiritual rest for yourself on a regular basis. Too many people build refreshment in their lives by sitting down to several hours of television a night, and by taking one or two vacations a year (similar to the one described above). Refreshment is much less effective when it is done sporadically and when it does not include all three areas—physical, psychological, and spiritual.

To further illustrate this vital truth, allow me to describe a typical day in the life of many people I have worked with over the years. They get up in the morning a bit sleepier than usual because they did not sleep well during the night. It takes extra caffeine in the form of coffee, Coke, or Mountain Dew to get their engines revving this morning. At work, they still do not feel quite awake, so they drink more caffeine and have a glazed donut at break in the hopes that a little refined sugar and carbohydrates will perk them up. At lunch, they are short on time, so they work at their desk and consume a bag of pretzels, a couple of Snickers bars, and a Pepsi.

By midafternoon, their energy is flagging, so they eat a chocolate chip cookie and wash it down with a can of Surge. Finally back at home at the end of the day, they sit down to a large dinner, have a second helping of dessert, and plop down sleepily in front of the TV. After the 10 P.M. news, they head off to bed feeling tired but agitated. They sleep fitfully again that night and wake up too tired to exercise the next morning, but promise themselves that they will start exercising again just as soon as they are through this crunch at work.

Does this routine sound familiar to you? At other times in my life, it was familiar to me. What I have come to recognize now is that physical, psychological, and spiritual refreshment are critically important in to my life on a daily or at least weekly basis. And it is important to get that refreshment in each of the three areas that we will now explore further.

Physical Jogging

The primary components of physical refreshment are eating, sleeping, and exercising. Most people sleep one to two hours less than they actually need at night. On the weekends or days off, they attempt to "catch up" on their sleep, only to discover that they generally feel groggy from getting too much sleep.

Your body will function optimally if you get the same number of hours of sleep each night. How much sleep is enough?

You can figure this out by taking three nights in a row when you do not need to get up at any particular time the next morning. On the first night, sleep until you wake up naturally without external aids like an alarm clock, kids, or noisy spouse. Do the same the second night. On the third night, note the time you began to drift off to sleep and the time you wake up without external aids. This is the amount of sleep you normally need per night. After days when you work particularly hard and are especially exhausted, you may need an addition 30 to 60 minutes of sleep.

Eating is an activity that sometimes is more psychologically refreshing than it is physically refreshing. Recently, my wife and I had dinner out with some friends and had a great evening of conversation, laughter, and stories. We also ate some really great tasting food. By the end of the evening, however, my stomach was getting upset from the amount and richness of the food I had consumed. I woke up several times during the night with stomach and intestinal cramps. The next day, I was tired and irritable. I had eaten more food than I physically needed, and too much of that food was overly rich in fats and sugars. From situations like this and from the various diet books I have been exposed to over the years, it is clear that eating a reasonable amount of food low in refined sugars and saturated fats and high in fiber generates the most physical refreshment when we are hungry.

Regular exercise is the third key to daily refreshment. Doctors and exercise physiologists will tell you as they have told me that the most important aspect of exercise is that it occurs on a regular basis. Walking for 20 minutes every day or even every other day is more refreshing than having a membership at a great health club that you rarely visit. Stretching and doing an exercise routine on your family room carpet three times a week is more effective than a workout room in your house fitted with weight machines and a stationary bike that you seldom use.

The truth about exercise is that those who do some level of it on a daily or every other day basis feel more awake and have access to better levels of energy than when they do not regularly exercise. The statistics also indicate that they tend to live longer and have greater mobility later in life than people who do not exercise.

Psychological Jogging

This type of refreshment includes any form of mental or emotional activity that creates a break in the intensity of normal activities. In many ways, psychological refreshment is similar to the function of the screensaver on your computer. My screensaver is the underwater scene that comes with many software programs, where bubbles rise to the surface and brightly colored tropical fish swim across the screen. These kinds of interesting images provide a psychological break that transports your mind and emotions to another place and time. They provide a psychological jog and renewed energy when you return to the task at hand.

Just as our bodies need to take physical breaks after prolonged periods of digging in the yard to install a retaining wall or shoveling snow to clear a driveway, our minds and emotions need breaks from an intense mental focus. We see evidence of this daily in situations all around us. Some of the most heartfelt laughter we ever experience comes after a funny story is recounted during the sadness of a funeral service. A highly stressful conversion to new software companywide generates some of the most creative humor and results in the sharing of favorite Dilbert cartoons. In the movie, *Life is Beautiful*, the main character creates a fantasy game to protect his young son from the real horrors of the Nazi concentration camp in which they are imprisoned. Each of these is an example of our natural tendency as humans to take psychological breaks as a way of refreshing ourselves.

Participants in my wholehearted leadership workshops have identified favored psychologically refreshing activities like these:

- Goofing off, sharing humor with coworkers, laughing
- Baking, cooking

- Doing yardwork, gardening
- Attending kids' sporting events
- Going fishing, camping, boating
- Riding a bike, motorcycle
- Hobbies
- Travel, getting out of town
- Entertainment, dancing, movies
- Dining out, long lunches with a friend
- Golfing, playing/watching sports
- Vacations
- Playing with kids, grandkids

Spiritual Jogging

Refreshing ourselves in this way requires us to be aware of our spiritual selves and to identify activities that awaken our spirits. Often, this occurs in the context of formal religious services. Aside from particular religious beliefs, however, it is clearly observable that certain activities tend to lift the spirits of human beings. Walking in natural surroundings, especially along an ocean, in the mountains, or at the edge of something like the Grand Canyon is an activity that profoundly affects our spirit. Listening to symphonic music, playing an instrument, or singing with a chorale can also have a huge positive impact on our spirit, as can activities like fasting, fervent prayer, quiet meditation, reading an uplifting autobiography, or viewing a movie about an inspiring character.

These are typical of the kinds of activities people have identified to me as spiritually refreshing:

- Taking a morning walk, taking long walks
- Viewing art in museums, churches
- Volunteering to help others
- Flying airplanes, gliders, hang gliding, parasailing
- Looking at flowers, gardening
- Listening to music, singing praise music at church
- Being on or near a lake, river, ocean
- Writing, painting, journaling
- Taking the time to daydream, read, enjoy a
  moment of quiet reflection
- Praying alone or in groups

The primary theme of these activities appears to be a connection with someone or something bigger than oneself. The
power and majesty of large bodies of water or mountainous
regions, the serenity of prayer or quiet reflection, the energized release of music, the beauty of flowers and natural surroundings, the love given and received in helping others—all
of these reflect the existence of an entity larger than our individual lives. As we feel the quiet presence of someone or
something larger than ourselves, it reassures us and lifts our
spirits. This is the essence of spiritual refreshment, and it is
something we need on a daily basis.

Some activities in our lives transcend any one of these three categories. Taking a hot bath and listening to uplifting music while the grandparents take the kids to an activity outside of the house could provide refreshment in all three areas. Spending a work break briskly walking through a beautiful grove of trees along a creekside path could also provide refreshment across all three.

It is critical to rest and refresh yourself throughout your week with adequate sleep, regular exercise, healthy diet, spiritual focus, and a mental break from work and the press of responsibilities. To refresh yourself in these ways daily and weekly is more powerful than several vacations per year. Failing to rest in these ways heightens your irritability, frustration level, feelings of entitlement, sense of "busy-ness," and inflexibility. Wholehearted leaders know the vital truth of regularly jogging themselves in these three ways, and they encourage those around them to stay regularly refreshed as well.

God, grant me the serenity to accept the things I cannot change, the courage to change the things I can, and the wisdom to know the difference.

—*origin uncertain*

8 | ACCEPT WHAT YOU CANNOT CHANGE, CHANGE WHAT YOU CAN

People in our culture struggle with the concept of accepting limits—that there are some things they cannot change. The United States grew under the rugged individualist banners of "Go West, young man," and "Pull yourself up by your boot-straps." We have learned from New Age/humanistic religion and philosophy that we need only to envision our future, believe in our own power, and assertively create our lives as we would have them be. Commercials exhort us to "Just do it" and to have "No fear."

We live in an age where people openly defy or ignore author-ity figures, where an almost limitless distribution channel called the Internet provides ungoverned communication, and where the emphasis is on pushing things to the extreme— extreme fashion, extreme sports, or extreme compensation for athletes and corporate executives. This emphasis on lim-itless freedom appears to have worked well for the new self-made and stock market-made millionaires and billionaires, but it leaves most of the rest of us rather self-conscious about the limits we seem to have in our lives.

The truth is that we all have limits. There are things we can control and things we cannot. Even people like Tiger Woods, Bill Gates, and Madonna have limits. The natural laws that govern our planet also impose limits such as gravity, the speed of light and sound, and the effects of the Earth's rotations. We have personal limits in our gifts and talents, our personalities, our motivated abilities, and our interests. There are some situations and people we can control, and some that we cannot. This belief in the natural occurrence of limits in life allows us to let go of trying to control everyone and everything and to trust that a positive outcome will occur.

Trying to control everything in your life is a frustrating, exhausting, and ultimately impossible task. To illustrate this point, George is a regional salesperson for a telecommunications firm. He has been with this company for 15 years and believes that he is management material, but has been passed over several times for such a role. Once in those years, he became a manager on an interim basis and it did not go very well. It is his fervent belief that he should be a manager; he suspects that his current manager disagrees with that conclusion and is doing everything she can to block his promotion.

It was helpful for George to distinguish between the results that he could control, and his wish to become a manager. Clearly, his objective of becoming a manager required the cooperation of his immediate manager, and the blessing of others in senior management. It seemed like the more George focused on trying to convince people he was management material, the further away he got from his goal.

When he recognized that this was a wish on his part that he alone could not make happen, his self-induced pressure began to ease. Instead, he was able to focus on achieving the results over which he had control. This shift in focus made George more successful at the tasks currently on his plate, and took the pressure off of his manager and other senior people so that they could look at him with a fresh eye when considering a management role down the road.

Wholehearted Leaders and Limits

Dean Buresh, executive vice president of Bozel New York, credits his ability to set limits to an uncle who told him early in life, "It doesn't do a lot of good to worry about things. Write down what worries you today and then look at what you have written in several weeks. When you do, you will realize that the thing you were worried about either did not actually come true, or it did come true but it was not the big deal you worried it would be. Besides, in the meantime you will have developed new worries to occupy your mind today."

In addition to this perspective from his uncle, Dean points to the importance of a sense of humor in order to laugh about or lighten up a situation. Often in crisis situations where the stress level is very high, Dean will impishly pose the questions, "Did anybody get killed today? Did we lose any body parts?" to provide realistic perspective on the extent of the problem. Most situations are just not that critical.

For Meghan Brown, limits are simply a matter of deciding "what is worth my energy and what is not," and recognizing that she has a limited amount of energy to expend every day. She knows her physical, mental, and emotional limits, and is aware of the symptoms when she is close to the edge. In her case, that usually means she begins to lose perspective and optimism, starts to feel anxious, and wants to sleep a lot.

Even with a generally optimistic attitude and a good sense of her own personal limits, Meghan finds herself crossing the line at times. At work, when she is involved with an issue about which she feels very passionate, she can "get hung up" and lose sight of her own limits. At home, particularly with her husband, Meghan sometimes has "a compelling need to be right," which can blur the line and make it difficult to let go of an issue. Both at work and home, her optimism helps set limits, because she often asks herself "Can we impact the outcome one bit by worrying?"

Barry Brottlund concurs, stating the most important lesson he learned along this line was not to overcommit his time.

He began learning this lesson during the years when his children were young, but continues to learn it today as he balances running his own business, spending time with his wife, and playing guitar and singing with several groups. Fortunately, his wife Sherry will remind him when they need to spend time together, and he responds by carving out time to be with her. "Busy-ness is the quiet and deadly thief of intimacy," he notes. "It doesn't slap you in the face, but it slowly erodes the time you need to sustain your most important relationships."

Together, Dave and Carol Graff recognize what they can control and what they cannot in many facets of their business lives. Dave, for example, used to be much more regimented in how he did his work—setting up structured times for cold calls, paperwork, and other details outside of his paid client work. "Now," he says, "if I'm not having a productive day, I don't try to fight it. One advantage of having your own business is the luxury of just taking time out to revitalize." That revitalizing time might include riding his motorcycle, hitting a few tennis balls, or taking a walk with their black Lab, Dude.

The bottom line for the Graffs is to recognize that they are not the ones in control when it comes to their business or their lives. "What it comes down to is that the Lord provides," says Dave. "We don't focus on the clients we don't have, we focus on the clients we have been blessed with. Somehow, we also see this as part of God's bigger plan. He opens and closes doors for us, and overall we're totally convinced that the business will be there as we need it to be."

Strategies for Serenity

One way to know the difference between what you can change and what you cannot is to distinguish between results and wishes. We can think of a "result" as *something you can achieve on your own,* like deciding to exercise three times a week or determining that you will thank at least three people each day who work with you. These are all results that you can focus on and accomplish on your own. On the other hand, a "wish" is *something that requires the help of others to achieve.* Examples of wishes include having a happy family, leading a high–performance work team, or enjoying a friendly relationship with your neighbors. Achieving any of these requires the cooperation and commitment of others.

Another way to set and accept naturally occurring limits is to apply the 80/20 rule. First, sort the issues that face you into two piles—those that you think you can change, and those that you think will be very difficult or impossible to change. Then, spend 80 percent of your time and energy trying to change the things you think you can affect, and only 20 percent of your time on those that you believe will be difficult or impossible to affect. As you work with issues, you may end up moving them from one pile to the other and changing the amount of energy you spend on each. The key is that you consider those you have control over and those you do not, and then use your wisdom and discernment to determine the difference between the two.

A third important aspect of setting limits is to forgive others who have hurt you or taken advantage of you in the past. Forgiving people is the way to set limits on how much the wrong they did to you will continue to cause you pain and suffering. When you forgive someone, you consciously decide to let them off your psychological hook. The major benefit to you of letting them off the hook—even though they may not deserve it—is to be able to let go of the hook you have been holding them on. It takes a great deal of energy to maintain an unforgiving attitude, and you will free up all that energy when you let go of the hook.

Forgiveness is a conscious decision of your head, followed by a peace in your heart. Forgiving people does not mean that you should forget what they did to you. Remembering what they did can help protect you from them or people like them in the future. Forgiveness is also a purposeful setting of limits. It is a way of recognizing the futility of trying to punish people by hating them for what they did. When you let them off your own personal hook, you can do it with the belief that they will ultimately be punished appropriately.

When a former business partner took advantage of me in our business relationship, I forgave him in my mind so I could let go of the hook, and turned his fate over to the marketplace. I firmly believed that someone with his business ethics would eventually be severely punished by the business community. After a time, I began to have compassion for the personal problems that led him to treat me the way he did, and then my heart forgave him as well. In other situations, I have taken people off my hook and turned them over to others with the belief that their friends/family would eventually punish them for their behavior. My most satisfying times of letting go of the hook have come as a result of turning these people over to a higher power, with the belief that God would look deep into their hearts and determine their punishment in his own time.

Life can only be understood backwards, but it must be lived forwards.

—*Søren Kierkegaard*

9 | ANSWERS TO BURNING QUESTIONS ABOUT VITAL TRUTHS

In discussing these concepts with individuals and groups over the past several years, a number of important questions have consistently been posed. Primarily, these questions have centered on how to live and lead wholeheartedly and how to better understand the dynamics between the seven vital truths. This last chapter presents some of those questions and attempts to provide answers.

Since every moment represents another opportunity to think about others, how do you think more about others and less about yourself without creating a continual and draining outward focus?

The attitude of thinking little about yourself and much about others is the most difficult of the seven vital truths. As I stated in Chapter 6, our culture encourages just the opposite through advertising and values centered on meeting our own needs. Because of that cultural context, it is difficult or impossible for us to imagine putting our focus on others right now. Consequently, we struggle with the notion and perhaps fight against it in our own minds.

The key is to remember that all seven truths are vitally important in the mix to create a wholehearted leader. It is better to believe and act according to all seven of these truths at a moderate level than to believe strongly in a couple of them and ignore the rest. There is a dynamic tension between these vital truths and a sense that the whole of them is greater than the sum of the individual truths. They tend to work together in ways that both balance and augment the others.

The three truths of focus on others, recognizing limits, and taking time for refreshment, for example, work very powerfully together to support a wholehearted attitude. It is impossible to focus one's attention on others right now all the time, because every new moment represents a new "right now." Totally focusing on others all the time would provide a quick recipe for burnout. But it must be developed in the context of some of the other truths—taking time for refreshment and recognizing limits. When focusing on others in your work and life outside work, it is critical to also take the time for psychological, physical, and spiritual refreshment, as well as to set reasonable limits for yourself.

One way to think about this dynamic tension in focusing as much as possible on others is to use the following as a guideline:

Focus your attention primarily on the needs of others in the moment, until your own need for refreshment becomes too strong or you recognize that you are no longer having a positive impact. If possible, bring the interaction to a close and find a way to return to the others' needs at a later time.

It is certainly easier for some people to focus on the needs of others. Those of us whose sense of purpose is something like "helping others to grow and develop" will likely be more energized by a consistent focus on the needs of others than someone with a very different life purpose. Further, if our motivated abilities include those of teaching, coaching, and counseling others, for example, we are more likely to be energized and enthusiastic through a consistent focus on others. To the extent that we are thankful for work that allows us to help others and optimistic about our capacity to affect a positive result, we are likely to sustain a focus that is primarily on others.

If thinking about the beauty that still remains means being completely content, where is the inclination to improve yourself and your life?

The key distinction in response to this question is that between thankfulness and complacency. To be thankful means to feel in your heart a sense of gratitude and to center your thoughts on how well your needs and desires are being met. If this were the only truth for living and leading wholeheartedly, you could envision a situation in which all your needs and desires were perfectly satiated and you just wanted your life to stay the same always. This would be a situation where there might be little or no inclination to improve your life or yourself.

The power of thankfulness, however, is experienced most clearly when all of your needs and desires have not been met. The joy of gratitude is experienced most powerfully when you are faced with areas of major need and want in your life. Being thankful in all things, in every circumstance, and focusing your attention on the ways in which your most important needs and desires have already been met—this is the essence of a thankful heart.

Furthermore, some of the other vital truths balance out any tendency toward complacency created by a thankful heart. Knowing the purpose in what you propose to do becomes a motor that drives your development. Most purpose statements that people have shared with me contain some element of getting better at something, becoming more effective, or growing and developing. Knowing the purpose in what you propose to do motivates growth and development for most people, particularly as it involves continually aligning your life to it. The vital truth of enthusiastic motivation also drives development. Knowing what your unique, innate talents are and wanting to use them and develop them further provides a counterbalance to complacency.

It takes a great deal of energy to be a wholehearted leader at work and at home; couldn't I just settle for "halfhearted leadership?"

It takes energy to do anything well. Developing a wholehearted attitude in the face of cultural pressure to be more self-focused and halfhearted takes time and effort. The beauty of developing a wholehearted attitude is that the attitude tends to build upon itself. That is, developing a strong belief and taking action based on any of these seven vital truths helps you grow more wholehearted in the other beliefs. The longer you work at developing wholeheartedness, the easier it becomes to keep your attitude permanently shifted and the less time you spend on it.

Further, the more wholehearted your approach with others, the more you create a space for them in which they can accept these vital truths and shift their own attitude toward greater wholeheartedness. The more their attitude begins to shift, the easier it is for you to continue to be a wholehearted leader around them.

This is exactly what happened with me in the context of my family. The more my attitude shifted toward thankfulness and optimism, for example, the more aware I became of my purpose in life and what gave me the greatest sense of motivation. I began to build in more time for refreshment on a regular basis, recognize my limits, and let go of many of my perfectionistic tendencies. I still need to work on thinking mostly of others when with my family, which means that I need to fight the urge to feel like I am off duty as a listener, coach, or developer of others when I am at home.

Is a wholehearted attitude enough to make someone an effective leader?

Effective leadership is the result of a combination of attitude, personality, and competence. Developing a wholehearted attitude across the seven vital truths provides a powerful foundation for effective leadership. Attitude is more fundamental than either character or behavior, and it drives the direction of both of these. But effective leadership requires more than a wholehearted attitude.

Being an effective leader requires knowledge, skill, and abilities in areas such as communication, problem solving and decision making, creating a vision, taking responsibility for results, and developing people. In fact, the model I often use in my executive coaching includes these twelve core competencies:
- Promote collaboration
- Listen with intent
- Communicate with integrity
- Value diverse perspectives
- Build competence and perspective
- Recognize critical implications
- Create innovative approaches

- Develop efficient systems
- Act on problems and opportunities
- Take responsibility for results
- Envision and communicate direction
- Influence and motivate others

Possessing these twelve competencies or others associated with leadership does not guarantee effectiveness as a leader. Effective leadership also requires that you lead comfortably within the boundaries of your personality. Some people are more confident being in charge, more drawn toward leadership positions, more assertive, more comfortable working with teams of people, and more flexible and adaptable. These and related personality characteristics lend themselves more readily to leadership roles, while other characteristics may make leadership a much more difficult role to play.

The key regarding personality is that you lead comfortably within the bounds of your style. Your approach as a leader must reflect a wholehearted attitude, a genuine expression of your personality, and an adequate level of effectiveness across core leadership competencies. If you have these seven truths firmly in your heart and mind, your attitude begins to shift to one of greater wholeheartedness.

All three of these components—personality, competence, and attitude—are important in being an effective leader. But if I had to choose just one of them as the most critical, it would be a wholehearted attitude. A wholehearted attitude is one that others will choose to follow, whether the setting is at work, at home, or in your community. And while your personality is relatively unchanging and competencies are often developed to an adequate level and then ignored, growing a wholehearted attitude based on these seven vital truths is the continuous work of a lifetime.

If you live your life by these vital truths, doesn't that just give others an opening to take advantage of you through their own self-focused tendencies?

This question does a great job of illustrating a common myth that I have encountered over the years in counseling and coaching people. The myth is that it is possible to protect yourself from the self-centered intentions of others by maintaining an attitude of guarded skepticism and distrust until you are sure you can trust them.

The problem with this type of thinking is twofold:

1. You tend to get more of what you focus on, and therefore create distrust.
2. Being guarded does not actually protect you from the attacks of others.

Let me explain this. People who are skeptical and guarded tend to create an environment around themselves that actually increases the likelihood of their being attacked in one way or another by others. It is a sort of self-fulfilling, self-defeating prophesy in which the more you distrust others, the more they distrust, devalue, and dislike you. That is, you tend to get more of what you have been focusing on and there is a greater likelihood of actually getting hurt.

Moreover, adopting a hypervigilant, guarded stance toward others in no way guarantees that you will catch them trying to harm you. Your guard may not be up at the moment they choose to use one of their self-focused destructive drives against you, unless you keep it up 24/7 to make sure nothing slips through the cracks. But if you are vigilant and protected all the time, you run the very real risk of interpreting someone's motives as intentionally hurtful when in fact they were intended to be helpful. When you interpret someone's positive motives as negative, it begins to foster a sense of distrust and dislike in them that may eventually come back to harm you.

Contrary to the thinking inherent in this question, the best strategy for protecting yourself from others is to create a bubble of wholeheartedness around you. Minimize your own self-focused tendencies, and instead, focus efforts every day on developing a wholehearted attitude by actively living out these seven truths. This will create a space around you that is characterized by trust, optimism, thankfulness, respect, and positive regard. This kind of a space will bring out the best in others, and you will waste little or no energy in a vain attempt to protect yourself.

What difference will knowing and living these vital truths actually make in my life?

This is perhaps the most difficult question to answer, since many of the changes in life are subtle and hard to trace to any particular source. Let me respond by first looking at the impact on my own life of living these vital truths.

Knowing the purpose in what I propose to do—to help people grow and develop—has helped me stay the course in my business when I've experienced a bad financial month or two, and kept me focused on spending my life's time primarily on what really matters. Also, I now understand that what energizes and motivates me is to have an impact on others by imparting the wisdom given to me, and I consistently use this in my aim to achieve great things. I know that the best work I will ever do is that which taps into my God-given talents, abilities, and gifts, and the more I fill my life with tasks that call upon these abilities, the more I will experience joy in my life's work.

Striving to think about the beauty that still remains has consistently focused my attention on situations and relationships that are going well in my life. As I thank God for the way I have been blessed in my life, for example, I find that my heart fills with gratitude and I naturally want to give some of it to others. The more I focus on the beauty in my life, the more I tend to express my gratitude to others around me at home, work, and church. Further, the more I find hope in the belief that things will get better, the more my optimism tends to create better things. These two truths about an attitude of thankfulness and optimism have done more than any others to significantly impact the quality of my life and my energy for living it.

Focusing on others by thinking less about myself and more about them has allowed me to be less overwhelmed by my own needs, desires, problems, and issues. It has also resulted in a much greater effectiveness in my work, and consequently much greater satisfaction with my work and life in general. The more I provide a role model for focusing on others, the greater the ripple effect on others around me that encourages and enables them to also think less about themselves and more about others.

But focusing on others every waking moment of our lives is an impossible and exhausting task. We need to jog ourselves physically, psychologically, and spiritually on a daily basis. When I determined how much sleep was optimal for me, committed to a regular exercise regimen, and recognized that at age 50 I could no longer eat food like I was age 25—I began to have access to much greater energy and vitality every day. When I recognized how important mental breaks and laughter were to keeping me energized throughout the day, I became even more wholehearted in my various life roles. And when I returned from a long hiatus to a strong set of spiritual beliefs and developed some discipline around these, the joy returned to my tasks and relationships.

The last vital truth that came to me was the importance of accepting limits—that there were situations and people I could change, and others that I could not. I learned that forgiving others was a critical part of recognizing my own limits. I learned that my acceptance of the fact that I was good at some things (speaking, writing), but not good at others (tuning up my car, handling finances, putting a deck on the house), was a healthy recognition that I could not change some things.

Perhaps the greatest insight and effect of these vital truths in my own life, however, came about as the result of my recognition that all seven of these truths must be believed and lived collectively. I began to see that they fed into and supported each other, and that any one or two of these truths lived fully could create problems without the existence of the others to counterbalance them. All seven are vitally important.

To fully answer this question, however, I sought a company

that would agree to send each of its employees through an experience in which they focused on these seven vital truths in their own lives. TAPEMARK, Inc. is such a company. They agreed to set up more than a dozen sessions, including some for early and late work shifts as well as exempt and nonexempt workers. Before the sessions began, each person filled out a pretest of 15 statements based on the vital truths and ranging from "I know my purpose in life," to "I put the needs of others ahead of my own," to "I let go of things that I cannot control."

Our hypothesis was that when given a posttest right after the session, people would score lower than on the pretest, but when given another posttest about 18 months later, they would score higher. Our reasoning was that after having been exposed to these seven truths, participants would recognize that they were not doing as well at living them on a daily basis as they could. Consequently, they would tend to score themselves more negatively right after the session.

This hypothesis was highly supported by the data. Of these 15 statements, 11 showed slight significance in lowered scores on the first posttest. The other four showed no significant change from the pretest. Clearly, people were grading themselves more negatively right after the session as they took a fresh look at their lives and recognized some issues that needed attention.

The second posttest, given almost 18 months later, mostly showed no significant change from the pretest. While this is a very slight move in the anticipated direction, it did indicate a slight rise in scores from posttest one to posttest two. That is, scores dropped below the pretest level on the first posttest, then rebounded to the pretest level on posttest two.

Only two of the 15 items showed a slightly significant increase from the first posttest to the second. These items were "I'm content with my needs being met in my life," and "I put the needs of others ahead of my own." The overall average score combining all items and all participants also showed a slight decrease on posttest one, and a slight increase from the pretest on posttest two. These overall average scores for the three testing periods—pre, post–one, and post–two—supported the hypothesis that scores would decrease slightly right after the workshop sessions, then increase as people began to build elements into their lives that were consistent with these vital truths.

These data do not clearly and unequivocally answer the question posed, but they do provide some support for the conclusion that when people live with a focus on these seven vital truths, their lives become better and their relationships improve. Though not much statistical significance was obtained, the "buzz" around TAPEMARK during and after these sessions clearly indicated strong positive feelings toward the organization for giving employees time to think about these things and share thoughts with coworkers. While it may have been coincidental, the United Way campaign held during the 18 months between posttests netted the highest total in the history of the company, and the number of days employees took off for sickness and other personal needs was reduced.

Several times in the body of this book you have referred to self-focused drives and irrational fears that get in the way of fully living these seven vital truths. What are these drives and fears, and how do they get in my way?

The answer to this question is much longer than space permits in this book. Look for my second book, *Lies, Drives, & Alibis* to be available sometime in 2003. In it, I discuss the destructive drives of self-focus, the irrational fears and faulty beliefs that push us into self-defeating reactions, and the lies we believe that provide a deadly anchor.

ACKNOWLEDGEMENTS

My heart is filled with gratitude for the many people who have influenced my life and provided the insight and anecdotes that compose this book. Growing up in Racine, Wisconsin, my parents—Don and Irene—encouraged creativity and modeled the love and commitment of a strong marriage. My brothers Brian and Barry, as well as my friends, helped me develop a sense of humor and a capacity to care about others. Later on in secondary school, teachers such as Jack Woodbury and Shirley Crull took a genuine interest in me as a person and encouraged me as a writer. Tremendous thanks to each of you, and to others not mentioned by name.

Thanks to the many friends and professional colleagues who have listened to me explain the concepts in this book, provided perspective, and encouraged me to write it. In particular, thanks to Bob Bemel, my friend and colleague, who after first hearing the vital truths of wholehearted leadership, exclaimed prophetically, "There's a book in there!"

Thanks to Bob Hardy, Betty Olson, Jim Warner, Dan Haag, Kerry and Mary Smith, Dave and Carol Graff, and members of the Faith at Work group for reading early drafts and providing helpful comments and suggestions. Thanks to my friends, professional colleagues, and members of my account-ability group for your great book title ideas and opinions. Thanks to the other wholehearted leaders quoted in the book—Dean Buresh, Barry Brottlund, Meghan Brown, Trudy Canine, and Rob Stevenson—for their willingness to be vulnerable and open in sharing their life and perspective with us. Thanks to my mother-in-law, Areatha Roby, for her daily prayers and unconditional support.

My deepest gratitude, however, goes to my wife and family. Thanks to Ben for his confidence in me, his unconditional respect and love for me, and his sense of humor that helps to refresh me when I most need it. Thanks to Kate whose gentle heart and firm convictions give me perspective, and whose sweet spirit and love lift me every time I come near them. But most of all, thanks to my beautiful wife Cindy who inspires me with her deeply held values and passion for giving, and who humbles me with her wholehearted love for me and unfailing commitment to our marriage. It was Cindy who took the risk of editing the very first draft of the manuscript and who has continued to provide valuable perspective and encouragement through the final decision on the title.

These people have provided nourishment to my heart and mind along way, but the true root of wholeheartedness in my life lies in my personal relationship with Jesus Christ. He who drew me in as a child—then let me wander aimlessly for 20 years in the desert of my own young-adult willful self-focus—now draws me close in a new way. I acknowledge that without his central presence in my life, my work and relationships would be halfhearted at best. I give him the glory for anything that I have accomplished or will accomplish in my life.

ABOUT THE AUTHOR

Bruce E. Roselle, PhD

A corporate psychologist who for 20 years has inspired clients with his breakthrough coaching, insightful assessment, and innovative facilitation and training, Bruce has worked with individuals and organizations in the public/nonprofit and private sectors ranging in size from entrepreneurial startup ventures to Fortune 100 companies.

He has written and cowritten articles that appeared in *Counseling and Human Development, the Executive Excellence* magazine, and the *Career Development Quarterly*. In addition, he has been quoted in newspapers, and magazines, and on radio and television on his views regarding creating work that is fun, dealing with stress at work, being aware of signs that your job is in danger, identifying personality characteristics that make individuals more hirable, and leading wholeheartedly.

A member of the American Society for Training and Development and the American Association of Christian Counselors, Bruce is past president of the Minnesota Career Development Association, and currently serves on its board of directors. He holds doctor of philosophy and master of arts degrees in educational psychology/counseling from the

University of Minnesota (1984, 1975). He earned his bachelor of arts degree in psychology from Northwestern University (1972).

Bruce lives in the Twin Cities in a little old house on the Mississippi River with his wife and two children. He can be reached by e–mail at **bruce@roselleleadership.com** and by snail mail at VitalTruths, P. O. Box 68, Anoka, MN 55303. Or, you can visit his website at www.roselleleadership.com